THE TRANSFER CHALLENGE

REMOVING BARRIERS, MAINTAINING COMMITMENT

HAROLD WECHSLER
Editor, Higher Education Publications
National Education Association

ASSOCIATION OF AMERICAN COLLEGES

THIS WORK WAS SUPPORTED BY
THE ANDREW W. MELLON FOUNDATION

Published by
Association of American Colleges
1818 R Street, NW
Washington, D.C. 20009

ISBN 0-911696-46-6

CONTENTS

FOREWORD

During the past three decades, the various components of the American educational establishment—elementary and high schools, community and junior colleges, and four-year colleges and universities—have tended to go their separate ways. In recent years, happily, there has been increasing recognition of the mutual advantages—indeed, the necessity—of cooperation among those segments. In a society in which work, civic participation, family life, and even leisure-time activity are increasingly knowledge-based, education is a necessity for all and not a luxury for a privileged minority. The improvement of education at every level, and the extension of its benefits to all, has become even more imperative in view of the increasingly competitive international economic and technological environment.

The aim of this handbook is to provide practical assistance to four-year institutions in their efforts to facilitate and increase the flow of students from two-year colleges into baccalaureate programs. As the handbook makes clear, the transfer traffic from the two-year colleges has been a very small stream, a surprising fact in view of the huge number of students—more than four and a half million—enrolled in two-year colleges. The practical lessons set forth in this handbook are derived largely from an AAC project that involved twelve four-year colleges and universities (eight independent and four public) and thirty-four community colleges.

I wish to thank the officers and trustees of the Andrew W. Mellon Foundation for the financial support that made the project possible and acknowledge the initiative and imagination of Mark Curtis, president emeritus of AAC, and Stanley Paulson, former vice president of the association, in designing the project. Jane Spalding, associate director of programs at AAC, directed the project with skill and followed its progress with penetrating insight. Harold Wechsler, author of this handbook, brought to his task historical discernment and a wide knowledge of the variety of cultures on American college campuses. AAC's director of public information and publications, Sherry Levy-Reiner, and her staff oversaw the production of this publication.

It is a pleasure to thank all those who had a role in the transfer project and those who have helped to make available to the entire higher education community the lessons that it has provided.

John W. Chandler
President
Association of American Colleges

PART ONE

COMMITMENT, COMPREHENSIVENESS, INSTITUTIONALIZATION

THE TRANSFER CHALLENGE

THE ROLE OF FOUR-YEAR INSTITUTIONS IN FOSTERING TRANSFER

REDUCING OBSTACLES TO TRANSFER

The American community and junior college movement is nearly one hundred years old. During this century, public and private two-year institutions have prepared millions of students for further academic studies and for the world of work.

Historically, many community and junior colleges viewed their primary mission as preparing students for transfer to four-year institutions for the last two years of baccalaureate study. Indeed, one measure of quality in a two-year college has been the percentage of the student body that does transfer.

Since World War II, however, the two-year college has undergone a major transformation that has complicated its historic commitment to transfer. In 1948, the President's Commission on Higher Education cited test results that showed most Americans to be capable of successfully completing fourteen years of education. The commission argued that economic and political changes required that Americans complete at least that many years of schooling. To meet this educational need, the commission called for growth in the number of two-year colleges, especially public institutions. These colleges would offer both general education for citizenship and vocational education for employment.

The community colleges dramatically expanded in size, numbers, and range of programs and community services. Today's community college caters to a multitude of community demands: for vocational and technical education, remediation, adult education, entertainment, liberal education, and transfer preparation.

We have an opportunity
to decrease the distance
between two-year and four-year institutions
and direct new attention
to facilitating transfer

Community colleges now are an important part of the American educational landscape. Community college expansion created unintended problems, however, for students who wished to transfer to four-year institutions. As the mission of the community college evolved to meet a broader range of needs, the earlier emphasis on liberal education and on the transfer function appeared to take a back seat to the newer demands. Community colleges rarely integrated new programs of vocational education with other offerings in liberal education. At many two-year colleges, moreover, the vocational mission eclipsed the emphasis on liberal education. As a result, many students in two-year institutions elected courses or programs that could not be applied toward baccalaureate programs in four-year institutions.

More recently, the proportion of the two-year college student population that *aspires* to transfer also has declined. This percentage always has been much greater than the percentage of students that actually transfer. Surveys show that before 1970 as much as three-quarters of a typical two-year college student body wanted to transfer. Of that number, less than half actually did transfer. Of today's five million matriculated community college students, notes Dale Parnell of the American Association of Community and Junior Colleges, perhaps a third now aspire to transfer; of that third, he adds, fewer than 20 percent do transfer. Other studies show that transfer aspirants often constitute less than half of the entering student body. The actual number of transfers from some community colleges may be less than five percent of the enrollees.

As transfer became only one of many competing missions within community colleges, four-year colleges and universities became more detached from the concerns of the two-year colleges. This detachment created additional obstacles for students who aspired to transfer from two-year to four-year schools.

American secondary education had followed a similar pattern earlier in this century. As secondary schools evolved from a "college preparation" mission to a more comprehensive mission, relations between secondary schools and colleges declined. The National Education Association's Committee of Ten, whose 1894 report influenced debates over the American high school curriculum for a generation, was composed of collegiate and secondary school representatives. Such a joint venture became infeasible after World War I. Between World War I and World War II, American high schools became "people's colleges," from which only a small fraction of graduates continued into higher education.

Formal and informal relationships between colleges and high schools declined. Colleges assumed full responsibility for determining their entrance standards and for determining who met those standards.

Only after World War II, as the proportion of high school graduates who went to college increased, did high school-college relationships improve—and then only in fits and starts—until now, when improving these relationships is much in vogue. The fact that improvement took this long suggests that without direct, constructive intervention it will take many years for two- and four-year college articulation, and the transfer function in general, to improve on their own.

Relations between two- and four-year colleges are in danger of following a course similar to the relations between secondary schools and four-year institutions after World War I. Diversification of their missions accompanied the relative and absolute increase in two-year college enrollments. Until the percentage of two-year college student transfers increases, facilitating transfer may not have a high priority at either two-year or four-year colleges. A chicken-egg situation would result: Colleges would wait for sufficient demand before attempting to increase transfer while the many barriers that impede transfer would inhibit formation of

sufficient demand.

Now, however, we have an opportunity to decrease the distance between two-year and four-year institutions and direct new attention to facilitating transfer. This opportunity arises in part from calls to restore general education to a central—indeed, for some critics, inescapable—position in the undergraduate curriculum. These calls draw attention to the role of liberal education in the community colleges and to community college programs that are a foundation for further study, and thus for transfer. Many two-year colleges have led the national review of the curricular effectiveness of the first two years of college.

Transfer also has come to the fore because many minority students are enrolled in America's two-year colleges. The "over-representation" of minority students in community colleges has led four-year institutions, whose own minority student populations declined during the 1980s, to take a closer look at transfer. Cutbacks in scholarships and grants, and perhaps racial strife at four-year colleges and universities, prompted minority students who otherwise would have gone to four-year institutions to enroll in less-expensive, "safer" community colleges. Facilitating transfer will help these students to continue their education and enable colleges and universities to address a conundrum that affects efforts to improve the status of minority students: the difficulty of reconciling "quality" and "equality." If removing transfer barriers leads to increases in both quality and equality, transfer will become a reform about which all parties may agree.

The issues of articulation, liberal education, and minority representation in the community colleges are much in the public eye. Recent reports on the future of the community college and on minorities in higher education highlight the transfer issue. Government, industry, and philanthropic foundations all take an interest in the transfer function. The Andrew W. Mellon Foundation and the Ford Foundation, among others, have allocated resources to many public and private institutions that are committed to breaking down barriers and devising improvements.

This handbook gleans general lessons from the experiences of twelve four-year colleges and universities and their two-year college partners in a project designed to facilitate transfer. These pilot programs sponsored by the Association of American Colleges and the Mellon Foundation revealed many important lessons about removing barriers to transfer that may result in widespread, permanent change.

One postulate is implicit throughout this handbook: Minority transfer from two-year to four-year colleges cannot be addressed fully without looking at the systemic problems that underlie it. Most of the five million two-year college students, whether minority or majority, simply cannot leave their institutions for another without a loss of time, credit, or both. Minority students, the AAC/Mellon project found, primarily benefit from targeted programs, but they also benefit from removal of the academic, economic, and social barriers that confront all transfer students.

Both public and independent four-year institutions derive rewards from confronting the curricular, economic, and bureaucratic issues that are involved in facilitating transfer. Independent colleges and universities receive greater numbers of students and an increasingly diverse student population; public four-year institutions fulfill their mandate to provide meaningful and effective access for all to higher education.

While the transfer question usually is seen primarily as a concern for liberal education, some of the largest undergraduate majors are vocational or professional: nursing, education, business, and computer science. Transfer is an equally important issue for students who major in these subjects. Indeed, many heated discussions of transfer deal with professional or vocational courses, since transfer barriers may include licensure requirements, accreditation issues, or external certification demands. The presence of huge numbers of minority students in career and vocational programs further fuels this debate. This report examines innovations in removing barriers in the area of liberal education. Many of the findings, however, are equally relevant to facilitating transfer of students with vocational or professional majors.

THE ROLE OF FOUR-YEAR INSTITUTIONS IN FOSTERING TRANSFER

This report is aimed primarily at four-year institutions. It is designed as a handbook for administrators and faculty members at such institutions who want to encourage community college graduates to matriculate in baccalaureate programs. The report recounts the history and results of a two-year demonstration project undertaken by AAC and funded by the Mellon Foundation. The project enlisted the resources of twelve four-year colleges and universities. Each institution chose one or more two-year colleges as partners in transfer facilitation. Eight of the four-year schools were independent institutions; four were public. All of the partner two-year colleges were public institutions. Participating four-

year colleges were chosen for their interest in transfer, for the merit of their proposals, and for geographic considerations.

During its two-year existence, the AAC/Mellon Transfer Project brought key project leaders together to share their findings and insights. This report is based on those insights, on the extensive documentation created during the project, and on follow-up discussions with key individuals in the participating two-year and four-year colleges and at AAC. The report also draws on the extensive literature on two-year college transfer.

The report focuses on how *four-year* colleges and universities can facilitate transfer. The choice of focus is dictated in part by AAC's membership. Ninety-seven percent of AAC's members are four-year colleges and universities or four-year colleges within larger universities. There are other reasons, however, why AAC seeks to alert four-year institutions—members and nonmembers alike—to its findings. Four-year institutions have an asymmetrical relationship with two-year colleges. When a four-year school changes its graduation requirements, it often sets a new standard for transfer admission. Two-year colleges that wish to facilitate transfer to that institution then must modify their own requirements to conform to the changes. The abil-

Reforms undertaken
to facilitate transfer
eventually must be institutionalized

ity of a four-year institution to act independently of external considerations is a prized aspect of American higher education, but it also may be a barrier to transfer.

The art of facilitating transfer consists of balancing coordination with institutional autonomy. Often this involves improvements in communications, expenditures of time and energy, and acceptance of some restrictions on a four-year institution's autonomy. The gains usually will outweigh the losses, but administrators who initiate programs to improve transfer must consider all consequences. Chapter Three of this report offers guidelines to four-year college presidents for facilitating transfer.

Our key recommendation is this: **Reforms undertaken to facilitate transfer eventually must be institutionalized.** A piecemeal approach, moreover—one that adopts only certain specific initiatives described in the following chapters—is insufficient. The recommendations in this handbook constitute more than a set of quick fixes. Their adoption involves serious institutional commitments to end the systemic problems that have emerged in the relations between two- and four-year colleges. Foundation support can facilitate these commitments. The most successful projects described in this report used AAC/Mellon funds (and the prestige

that came with the money) first to experiment and then to institutionalize the results of those experiments. Foundation grants, however, are not a substitute for institutional commitments.

The need to institutionalize reform is especially urgent in facilitating the transfer of minority students. Some observers now are optimistic that minority enrollments in the nation's colleges and universities, after several years of decline, again will increase. On the other hand, minority enrollments may increase temporarily in any fall—when colleges, responding to numerous exhortations, devote additional resources to minority recruitment. Reforms always may be undone, however, unless they are institutionalized. The problems attendant upon minority recruitment are deep-seated and require serious thought about resources and consequences over more than one or two academic years.

Let us immediately anticipate a possible objection to our key recommendation. Commitments must, of course, be personal, not only institutional. Indeed, many project directors report that the creation of personal relationships was absolutely vital to the success of their projects. The continual creation of such personal relationships and the continual creation of commitment are two important aspects of transfer that must be institutionalized. We also believe that responsibility for transfer must be placed in the hands of more than one individual, however committed that individual may be to facilitating transfer. Dispersal of responsibility assures that the reassignment or departure of any one person does not place an entire system of reforms in jeopardy. Such dispersal also facilitates creation of the comprehensive effort that is required to address the systemic issues we identify.

REDUCING OBSTACLES TO TRANSFER

What precisely is "transfer"? What are the barriers to transfer? Transfer is admission from one institution to another and the acceptance of course credits already earned by the student who is transferring. Transfer can be from a two-year college to a four-year college or university, from one four-year institution to another, from a four-year college to a two-year college, or from one two-year college to another. This handbook addresses the issues involved in transfer from two-year to four-year colleges, but many of the same considerations apply in the other three instances.

The literature on transfer identifies numerous barriers to transfer between two- and four-year colleges.[1] We may summarize these under

seven main headings:
☐ Academic and articulation barriers
☐ Inadequate support systems
☐ Economic barriers
☐ Bureaucratic barriers
☐ Geographic barriers
☐ Age impediments
☐ Racial and ethnic concerns.
Both traditional and minority students are affected by the first six barriers, though often to different degrees.

Academic and articulation barriers
All too often, students embarking upon their studies at a new institution discover that the courses they completed elsewhere will not be counted toward their new school's general-education, major, or other graduation requirements. In this context, articulation—a key aspect of transfer—means continuity in coursework within and between institutions. The new institution expects that a student's mastery level in the completed courses will be sufficient for the student to begin the next course in its sequence. Many attempts at transfer facilitation fail over the issue of articulation. Department chairs or individual instructors may be suspicious of work completed elsewhere and may require transfer students to complete coursework similar to their work at the previous institution. Students of-

ten find that while they have been accepted to a four-year college or university and have gained degree credit for their completed work, they are not considered to have completed various qualitative degree requirements.

As a result, students who arrive at four-year institutions with an associate of arts degree that presumably represents two years of work find they must complete far more than two additional years of work to obtain their baccalaureate degrees. A large-scale study of community college students who transferred to the University of California–Los Angeles between 1976 and 1978 found that transfer students took an average of 1.4 years longer to obtain the baccalaurate than those who had begun their college careers at UCLA.[2] While many factors may explain such differences, the fact that many transferred credits are counted as elective credits rather than as required credits often is a significant barrier to transfer. Many students do not bother to make the effort.

Conversely, four-year institutions often accept two-year college students before these students complete their associate of arts degrees. This may help an individual student save some time, but two-year colleges often object that such "raiding" deprives them of their best students, that it reduces their ability to offer

sophomore-level courses, and that it is a disincentive to their cooperating with the "raiding" college.

Articulation agreements usually are seen as the solution to these problems. These agreements allow students to complete their work at the two-year college and allow that work to meet general-education and major requirements at the four-year institution. Such agreements, however, often are difficult to negotiate because considerations of institutional autonomy may outweigh the need for compromise on all sides. Even when they exist, articulation agreements quickly can become outdated. State-mandated articulation policies, when they exist at all, often are unenforced and weak.

Inadequate support systems

Four-year college admissions officers usually are more accustomed to working with high school students than with two-year college transfers. While they are cognizant of general trends in secondary education and of specific conditions at feeder high schools, they often are unaware of broad developments at two-year colleges and activities at potential feeder colleges. Many colleges sponsor minority recruitment programs aimed at local high schools, but few such programs are aimed at two-year college minority students.

Potential transfer students often

are inadequately counseled. At many large community colleges, students register just before classes begin. They have little chance to meet any college representative, save for a registration clerk. Faculty counseling at two-year colleges rarely is a strong point, and it becomes more sporadic when institutions replace full-time faculty members with part-timers to cut costs. Students approach faculty members, if at all, when options already are lost. (The student-faculty relationship is especially important because at many two-year colleges faculty members do most student advising and sometimes are contractually obligated to do so.)

Counseling is extremely important for potential transfer students, in part, because of the student culture at two-year colleges. The student culture often is vocationally oriented. Students cushion themselves against disappointment by remaining aloof from formal institutional goals. Even officials with the best of intentions may have difficulty getting capable students to think about, much less to work toward, transfer. The norms of this culture help explain why community college attrition rates are high. One four-year institution with an excellent track record in transfer experienced many difficulties in recruiting minority students for a special program under the AAC/Mellon grant. When questioned, potential recruits described an unsupportive student culture.

Observers discern improvement in four-year college orientation programs for transfer students. They conclude, however, that these improvements do not offset declines in services to two-year college students brought about by enrollment increases and the shift to a part-time teaching force.

Economic barriers

Two-year colleges are populated by students who often are dependent upon federal and state financial aid programs. The shift in federal programs to an emphasis on loans instead of grants means that these students will accumulate large amounts of debt and therefore may be discouraged from considering transfer. While the "portability" of federal grants has helped many transfer students, state financial aid policies do not work uniformly to their benefit. Finally, the high tuition charges of private colleges and universites often hinder transfer.

Bureaucratic barriers

Bureaucratic issues compound the academic, support, and economic problems. Admissions policies and procedures often are problematic. Two-year college students, especially part-time students, are accustomed to registering at the last minute, af-

Minority students confront all the barriers
faced by nonminority students
plus barriers brought about by decades
of discrimination and indifference
to their educational needs

---

ter determining what their employment and family obligations will allow. The complex admissions procedures for transfer often must be completed months—not hours—in advance. Transfer students may find they have missed unalterable deadlines because they were unaware of or unconcerned about them. Deadlines are a major problem at the more selective and independent institutions that employ multiple criteria for admission.

A second problem is that information may be unavailable. Many four-year institutions do not publish materials aimed at transfer students from two-year colleges. Others publish general information but do not indicate which two-year college courses meet specific degree requirements.

Few institutions collect data about two-year college transfer students. Two-year colleges usually do not know the academic fate of their students once they graduate or transfer. Four-year colleges and universities often do not single out transfer students for data collection. Many institutions do not know whether their transfer students fare better or worse than "native" students.

Geographic barriers

Community colleges often are precisely that: institutions that are visible within and offer multiple services to a locality. Four-year colleges and universities may be geographically remote precisely because their founders wished to isolate them from the attractions and distractions of urban life. Students sometimes overlook remote four-year institutions that are willing to accept students from two-year colleges. Students who do transfer may find that the small towns that surround these schools may not reflect the demographic composition of their home communities. When urban and minority students feel unwelcome, a geographic barrier can be translated into a sociological or a psychological barrier.

Age impediments

Many community colleges enroll large numbers of older students. Neighboring four-year colleges and universities may ignore these students when contemplating transfer facilitation. Older students have family and economic responsibilities that may prevent them from participating fully in campus life. They require different kinds of counseling, course scheduling, and financial aid. Many four-year institutions do not consider applications from students whose age exceeds a predetermined cutoff.

Racial and ethnic concerns

The disproportionate enrollment of blacks, Hispanics, and other minority students in two-year colleges poses a substantial challenge for four-year institutions that wish to enroll students from these populations. Forty percent of all black college students are enrolled in two-year colleges. Fifty-three percent of Hispanic and native American students choose two-year institutions. In contrast, 32 percent of all white students opt for two-year colleges.[3] Transfer aspirations, moreover, are greater among white than among minority students.

Minority students confront all the barriers faced by nonminority students plus barriers brought about by decades of discrimination and indifference to their educational needs. Many minority students view local community colleges as nearby, affordable institutions that offer vocational programs leading to immediate employment. Four-year colleges and universities that wish to draw upon this population to compensate for their own declining minority enrollments will have to demonstrate an interest in minority students and a relevant academic program.

Different types of institutions confront these barriers differently. Within each institutional type, campuses vary in their sophistication and experience in dealing with transfer. Some colleges offer only junior- and senior-level instruction and rely on transfers for their entire student body. In contrast, some four-year institutions accept few transfer students, whether from two-year colleges or from other four-year schools.

This handbook examines public and independent four-year colleges and universities, describes the barriers these institutions must confront, and identifies actions that they can take to reduce or eliminate these barriers. Our accounts reflect differences in experience among grant recipients as well as differences among institutional types.

The fate of relations between two-year and four-year colleges need not follow the pattern of high school and college relations set earlier in this century. Indeed, many institutions in the AAC/Mellon project successfully reversed declines in the number of students transferring; others successfully recruited minority students. In addition, these schools created a salutary environment for the investigation and resolution of other issues of mutual concern. While liberal arts study and transfer preparation may no longer be the sole, or even the central, missions performed by two-year colleges, they still significantly affect all that goes on at the two-year college. This handbook shows how transfer facilitation may help foster a resurgence in cooperation between two- and four-year colleges and promote equity for minority students.

■

THE AAC/MELLON TRANSFER PROJECT

AAC's proposal to the Andrew W. Mellon Foundation listed two objectives:

☐ uncovering and overcoming the barriers to transfer
☐ maintaining four-year college enrollments.

The proposal emphasized minority access. It noted that, controlling for ability, minority students who enter community colleges have lower baccalaureate degree completion rates than do minority students who enter directly into four-year institutions.

The proposal built upon a 1983 survey conducted among AAC-member institutions. The survey found that one-third of AAC's member institutions actively recruited transfer students from two-year colleges and viewed them as an important source of enrollments. One-third of these active recruiters had no formal articulation agreements with two-year colleges. Of the colleges that did not recruit transfer students, one-third indicated they were considering a policy change.

The survey identified five areas that needed special attention:

☐ compatibility of curricula
☐ requirements in foreign languages
☐ availability of financial aid
☐ judgments on academic ability of students
☐ faculty attitudes.

AAC proposed to select some institutions with success in transfer, some whose efforts resulted in sporadic success, and some that had not previously attempted transfer recruitment but intended to do so. The twelve pilot program sites included three universities, three comprehensive institutions, and six liberal arts colleges. There were eight independent and four public institutions.

The independent schools were:

☐ Clark College; Atlanta, Georgia. A member of the Atlanta University

Successful transfer requires the involvement of more than one or two faculty members

Center, Clark is a predominantly black institution that enrolls 1,860 students.

☐ Jacksonville University; Jacksonville, Florida. An independent college founded in 1934 as a junior college, Jacksonville enrolls 2,214 students.

☐ Kalamazoo College; Kalamazoo, Michigan. Founded in 1833 and historically affiliated with the American Baptist Convention, Kalamazoo enrolls 1,103 students.

☐ Knox College; Galesburg, Illinois. A residential, independent college, Knox enrolls 967 students.

☐ Occidental College; Los Angeles, California. Founded in 1887, Occidental is a residential college that enrolls 1,649 students.

☐ University of Miami; Coral Gables, Florida. A doctoral-granting institution founded in 1925, Miami enrolls 15,929 students.

☐ University of Puget Sound; Tacoma, Washington. An independent college affiliated with the United Methodist Church, Puget Sound enrolls 2,954 students.

☐ Vassar College; Poughkeepsie, New York. Established as a college for women in 1861, Vassar became coeducational in 1969. The college enrolls 2,319 students.

The public institutions were:

☐ California State University–Hayward; Hayward, California. Chartered in 1957, California State University–Hayward is a unit of the state university system. Located near Oakland, the university enrolls 12,373 students.

☐ Temple University; Philadelphia, Pennsylvania. A state-related institution founded in 1884, Temple is a doctorate-awarding institution that enrolls 31,471 students.

☐ University of Arizona; Tucson, Arizona. A state institution and land-grant college, Arizona enrolls 31,569 students.

☐ University of Massachusetts–Boston; Boston, Massachusetts. Founded in 1965, the University of Massachusetts–Boston is a commuter institution that enrolls 12,919 students.

AAC asked each selected institution to agree to a set of "Formal Conditions of Institutional Participation." These conditions assumed that successful implementation of a transfer program required improved communication among institutional counterparts (administrators, faculty members, students, and support personnel). The "Formal Conditions"—based on the research on transfer completed through 1984—specified a set of internal actions for participating colleges and universities. The four-year institutions would create five kinds of working relationships with area two-year colleges. We list these sets of relationships here, along with a brief commentary on the rationale for inclusion and on our findings about these relationships.

☐ *Formal arrangements for consultation and procedures for concluding agreements among presidents and chief academic officers of both the four-year institution and the two-year college or colleges involved.* AAC and Mellon had viewed presidential participation as crucial. Little that happened over the following three years has led AAC to change its views. Some important successes resulted from presidential leadership. Some of the most notable shortcomings occurred when it was absent.

☐ *Provision for regular meetings among admissions officers, academic counselors, and financial aid officers within the four-year institutions and meetings with counterparts at the two-year colleges.* This presupposed that informal contacts were necessary, if not sufficient, for regularizing a transfer relationship. In several cases, personal interaction strengthened the institutional relationships, especially when it was actively cultivated by both sides. Occasionally, however, creation of informal relationships was allowed to replace, rather than complement, more formal arrangements. The project also revealed that the relevant officials who deal with transfer on the four-year campus often fail to interact regularly with each other.

☐ *Formal and informal exchanges between the faculties of the four-year and two-year colleges so that faculty members at each institution learn first-hand about the academic programs on the other campus or campuses.* Once faculty members actually get together and talk, many barriers crumble. Collegial relationships and informal communications between counterparts permit discussions about individual students and their needs as well as about the content of courses. A small four-year college dealing with one or two two-year institutions probably can rely on informal relationships to a greater extent than can a comprehensive public university. Informal relationships end, however, when a colleague departs for another institution or retires. Successful transfer requires the involvement of more than one or two faculty members.

☐ *Opportunity for students from cooperating institutions to spend time on one another's campuses, talk with other students, and attend classes.* Two-year college students should become acquainted with the environment and programs of the four-year college or university. At the same time, transfer students from two-year colleges who are successful at the four-year school make excellent models for other two-year college students. Some programs devoted little attention to student visitation, but one successful program considered it crucial. The directors of that program assumed that prior exposure to a radically different environment might diminish misconceptions, reduce "transfer shock," and increase the attractiveness and desirability of transfer.

□ *Regular consultations between staffs of learning development centers to share information and understanding of the special characteristics, attributes, problems, and needs of transfer students in order to improve their opportunities and performance on both kinds of campuses.* AAC took seriously the notion that research and practice have produced understanding about the cognitive and affective development of students in general and transfer students in particular. Save for one institution, however, the four-year colleges and universities in the AAC/Mellon project did not take such understandings into account, although they said they would. Even if inclined to do so, few administrators have the time to master this research, much less plan on its systemic incorporation into a well-conceived transfer program. When individual faculty members took on the developmental and nurturing role discussed in this literature, transfer was facilitated.

AAC established no formal consortium, although it did bring project directors together for several meetings. Nor did AAC attempt to define overall standards for transfer. In-

deed, AAC expected some four-year institutions to take minimal steps toward transfer facilitation rather than implement a full transfer plan. The 1983 survey indicated that some of the participating colleges and universities could do little more in two years than seriously think about transfer and take some initial steps.

Participant institutions enhanced transfer by devoting attention and resources to the "Formal Conditions." AAC found, however, that lasting success in removing barriers required more systemic thinking. It is one thing to exhort faculty members; it is another to create the environmental conditions that allow favorably predisposed faculty members, who often are pulled in many directions at once, to act on their good intentions. The transfer process must be seen as a whole. Responsible officials must determine how transfer fits in with other institutional agendas and how to accomplish the permanent removal of transfer barriers within the limits of institutional resources and interest.

The AAC/Mellon Transfer Project demonstrated that imposing the "Formal Conditions for Institutional Participation" fostered closer ties between two- and four-year college counterparts and was a salutary step, but it was only a part of a larger story. The reports of the twelve participants suggest three principles that are critically important to transfer facilitation. Conceptually these principles are independent of each other. AAC found, however, that in practice the most successful programs exhibited all three principles. The presence of these principles did not *guarantee* success, but their presence *maximized the probability* of attaining it. (The availability of resources also affected the probability of attainment.) These principles are listed here and discussed in detail in the next chapter.

□ *Commitment.* Leaders at both four-year and two-year colleges had to recognize the importance of transfer to both their students and their institutions. Commitment had to begin at the top. Faculty members and administrators who initiated and implemented reform then would be secure in the knowledge that the institution stood behind them. Initiatives not based on such commitment went nowhere.

□ *Comprehensiveness.* Initiatives taken in one area usually had far-reaching effects. Improved counseling, for instance, might affect faculty members, financial aid, staff members, and other students. The most successful programs considered all potential effects of their multiple, integrated initiatives. Strong, committed leaders facilitated an integrated response.

□ *Institutionalization.* Informal relationships are necessary for the initiation of successful reforms. For the perpetuation of these programs, however, reforms had to be institutionalized. Personal relationships counted for much, but when key faculty members or administrators changed positions—which happened often during the project—entire initiatives were placed in jeopardy. Conversely, institutionalization permitted the emergence of new personal relationships.

While the dollar amount of the AAC/Mellon grants was not large, the successful programs invested their funds to assure commitment, comprehensiveness, and institutionalization. The grants could not substitute for the institutional commitment of resources, but they did allow for planning for the most efficient use of those resources.

RECOMMENDATIONS

FOUR-YEAR INSTITUTIONS

TWO-YEAR INSTITUTIONS

There are many ways to improve transfer between two- and four-year institutions. Improving faculty communication, creating better data bases, coordinating student services, creating specific articulation agreements, encouraging student visits, and increasing financial aid—all of which were undertaken by AAC/ Mellon project participants—will facilitate transfer. Removing barriers that have been built up over many years takes time, however. Some institutions laid groundwork for the future rather than emphasizing immediate enrollment increases. Many barriers to transfer result from fundamental changes in the mission of two-year colleges that neither two-year nor four-year institutions can reverse. Partner schools, however, can see that potential transfer students are not disadvantaged as a result of these changes.

In this chapter, we discuss the principles that underlie successful and sustained implementation of the individual suggestions. AAC believes that institutions should plan care-fully before adopting any of the suggestions offered in Part Two of this handbook. Removing barriers only temporarily may be worse than not removing them at all, since any second attempt at removal will come up against memories of the first failure—as well as the barriers themselves.

We begin with a discussion of commitment, comprehensiveness, and institutionalization. We then comment on how the two-year college partners may help assure the permanent removal of barriers.

FOUR-YEAR INSTITUTIONS

Commitment. Commitment to breaking down transfer barriers should be broad-based and sustained. Lasting commitments must begin with an institution's top leaders. In the successful AAC/Mellon projects, presidential involvement allowed staff members to proceed with the knowledge that their work would be supported and rewarded.

Each institution in the AAC/ Mellon project committed its own

Commitment to breaking down barriers
should be broad-based and sustained.
Lasting commitments must begin
with an institution's top leaders

---

resources. Indeed, presidents must make a cost/benefit calculation whenever they contemplate a significant commitment of resources. AAC asked four-year college presidents to assess their situation realistically before embarking on transfer facilitation. Neither lip service nor backing off from commitments once made is conducive to the long-term enhancement of transfer. The following list of considerations is based upon the reports of the twelve four-year institutions in the AAC/Mellon project.

☐ What is the demography of local community colleges? Are there significant numbers of students who might transfer? Does my institution directly compete against potential two-year college partners for first-year students? How will these colleges view our overtures?

☐ Is the initiative to be undertaken simply to garner community good will, or is the program to be integrated into the institution's ongoing mission?

☐ Who on my faculty and staff will support an initiative? Who will oppose it? Will I support faculty members who teach jointly with two-year college faculty members and negotiate articulation agreements? Do I have personnel on my staff with the interest, knowledge, time, and commitment to make the initiative work? What must be given up? Will fewer recruiters go to target high schools?

☐ What are the initiative's apparent and hidden financial costs? Is there scholarship money available to support transfer students? (At a minimum, financial aid policies should not penalize transfer students.)

☐ Is the program primarily geared toward increasing minority enrollment or increasing transfers? Are there more cost-effective mechanisms to increase minority enrollments? Which actors should be brought into the initiative? (There is a tendency to confuse goals of a transfer initiative. Different personnel may be required depending on the ultimate goal.)

A president should make commitments only after wide consultation with appropriate faculty and staff members. Once the president has made and demonstrated a commitment to see a project through, other commitments may be elicited. For example, presidents may look for a concern with transfer issues when appointing a candidate to a department chair.

A presidential commitment means an investment of adequate institutional resources. Presidents may provide released time and other resources necessary to officials responsible for transfer. Delegating responsibility to an admissions or other administrative officer alone, however, is problematic. These officers usually cannot enlist the faculty assistance that is vital for transfer success. Furthermore, involved faculty members will need to be relieved of other duties if they are to make transfer a priority, and many staff members cannot make the necessary commitments.

A committed president must participate in activities that facilitate transfer. A single meeting with community college counterparts may yield only symbolic good will, not substantive change. Four-year college presidents must guard against creating resentment among two-year institutions that assign higher ranking officials to important transfer roles.

Comprehensiveness. Once a four-year college or university is committed to facilitating transfer, it must design a comprehensive policy. Some AAC institutions began with piecemeal efforts. Academic leaders at these institutions believed that some parts of their institutions were more easily mobilized than others. Thus, some AAC/Mellon projects emphasized increased faculty cooperation; others emphasized the creation of brochures, handbooks, and course guides; and still others emphasized improved support services. These salutary initiatives might remove individual barriers to transfer. Piecemeal efforts, however, rarely yield sustained results or change the underlying situation. An institution that emphasizes only one barrier may not

correctly identify the *key* barrrier—if such a single barrier exists at all.

Initiatives in one area have implications in many other areas. Thus, better counseling can occur only if departmental faculty members have clear policies on transfers for the counselors to convey. The experiences of Vassar College and California State University–Hayward, described in Part Two of this handbook, demonstrate the importance of regular meetings of all concerned personnel. These meetings should occur both within the four-year institution and between the two-year and four-year colleges.

Comprehensive, coordinated programs that address all barriers have the greatest chance for success. Each part of an institution should know what the others are doing about transfer, and some individual or group should know everything that is going on.

An institution's attitude toward negotiations, even over small matters, is crucial to the success of an initiative. Four-year schools must recognize quality in community college students and community college offerings. Two-year colleges must recognize the goal of coherence in the four-year college curriculum. Discussion of problematic issues, such as skills prerequisites, course equivalencies, the integrity of associate degrees, acceptability of D grades, and credit for repeated courses, should proceed from positions of candor, trust, and mutual respect.

Institutionalization. Commitment to transfer should result in routine contacts between the four-year institution and its two-year college partners. A presidential commitment must be translated into working relationships between institutional counterparts. Especially in the case of public institutions, this translation implies formal arrangements to accommodate the hundreds of transfer students that graduate from the larger community colleges. Everything need not be done at once. Indeed, some four-year college officials will find it difficult to determine their counterparts at partner two-year colleges. The successful AAC/Mellon four-year schools that began with little or no experience in transfer did not jump in with both feet. Their initial efforts were modest building blocks toward further facilitation.

A four-year college or university can undertake many steps even before approaching potential two-year college partners. The four-year college president may work with concerned officials to review current practices: academic, financial, counseling, and other support. The president should stress the key role of academic officials. Without the cooperation of department chairs, for instance, efforts to improve transfer

may go nowhere. Some steps—such as publishing a clear transfer policy in the college catalog—may be taken immediately. Informing students about institutional policies for the transfer of credit clarifies these policies internally and leads the institution to follow its own stated procedures.

Putting one's own house in order facilitates an institution's approaches to two-year colleges that might otherwise be skeptical. To be specific: A proposal for dual enrollments should not precede clarification of the catalog. Nor should a four-year institution negotiate a general articulation agreement until after it has developed course-by-course equivalencies. Otherwise, its own faculty members may be reluctant to accept the general agreement.

A formal agreement with a partner demonstrates a commitment and concern that will lead to further initiatives. The agreement also may be used as leverage with other institutions. For example, Broward Community College officials used their agreement with Clark College to negotiate similar agreements with two four-year colleges in Florida.

An independent institution that ventures into transfer may find that potential partners already participate in working relationships and articulation agreements with other (usually public) colleges. One independent four-year institution found that it had to conform to extensive articulation agreements between two- and four-year public colleges or opt out completely. One community college, notes an administrator, participated in the AAC/Mellon project primarily to educate its four-year college partner about the financial obstacles that potential transfer students encounter. This community college already participates in a state compact for transfer among public institutions and has two prior agreements with other independent colleges.

Independent colleges and universities that enter transfer agreements with an eye toward enrollment increases may face competition from institutions that have eliminated barriers to transfer. A public college or university that is governed by a weak articulation agreement (one that facilitates admissions but allows few credits toward the bachelor's degree and few course equivalents) may feel the competition from an aggressive private institution.

Conversely, a four-year college or university that "gets there first" may set the parameters for agreements that two-year partners later sign with other four-year institutions. A University of Miami agreement with Miami-Dade Community College called for admission to the junior class with general-education requirements fulfilled (instead of using course-by-course equivalencies). Soon after, four other institutions negotiated similar agreements.

Shortcomings both within and outside the AAC/Mellon project frequently resulted from turnover in faculty members or administrators with responsibilities for transfer. Especially in larger institutions, transfer cannot rely indefinitely on informal relationships between administrative or faculty counterparts at partner institutions. Many AAC/Mellon project successes did begin with informal contacts. The presence of spouses of Vassar College faculty members on the Dutchess Community College faculty, for instance, facilitated communication between Dutchess and Vassar. The most successful projects, however, began to regularize and perpetuate informal contacts as part of their long-term strategies.

The growing number of part-time faculty members at both two- and four-year institutions is a major barrier to enhancing transfer. Revolving-door faculty members cannot create many informal contacts. Nor can they counsel students, much less make academic commitments on behalf of an institution. Increasing the proportion of full-time faculty members will go far toward eliminating confusion among students as they seek advice in navigating the maze of transfer requirements.

TWO-YEAR INSTITUTIONS

The principles listed above generally apply to four-year colleges and universities that wish to break down barriers to transfer. Additional lessons derived from post-project explorations with leaders of two-year campuses apply to two-year colleges:

☐ Gauge your own and your partner's experience with transfer. A community college that has sophisticated relationships with some four-year institutions may have to shift gears when dealing with a four-year college that is new to transfer.

☐ Plan well in advance to assure that courses are offered in the necessary subjects to guarantee not only transfer but acceptance of these subjects toward the four-year institution's general-education requirement. Acceptance requires staffing sophomore-level courses that often are left to wither for lack of enrollments. A two-year college that develops a reputation for facilitating transfer may experience greater future enrollments in these courses.

☐ Examine policies on the use of part-time faculty members. The excessive use of part-time faculty members by two-year colleges may raise suspicions among four-year institutions about the quality of two-year college course offerings.

☐ Plan to identify and counsel transfer students as early as the first semester of the freshman year. Transfer representatives from four-year institutions should assess potential applicants while they are still at the two-year college.

☐ Strive for an open relationship with the four-year college partner. Many two-year college representatives will forgo partnerships if a four-year institution recruits many students who have not finished their courses of study at the community college. Express feelings about such premature transfer tactfully but candidly. Remember that four-year colleges and universities also may see two-year colleges as competitors for first-year students. If both sides fail to assess possible gains and losses from cooperation, key actors will fail to attend meetings, perform necessary implementation, and institutionalize gains. That is, they will vote with their feet.

Eliminating barriers to transfer is an opportunity and a responsibility. Beginning a commitment with a symbolic gesture may be important. The removal of long-standing barriers, however, requires commitment, comprehensiveness, and institutionalization of reform. Not all schools will adopt transfer facilitation initiatives, nor should they. A true commitment presupposes affirmative answers to some difficult questions, but the institutional culture of more four-year and two-year institutions should allow for transfer. In turn, facilitating transfer will encourage two-year and four-year colleges to work together on other issues of common concern.

Federal and state programs and institutional commitments have helped high school students overcome many barriers to college access. The recent growth of community colleges and the attendant quality and equity considerations require that postsecondary educators assure that the baccalaureate degree becomes attainable by all capable students.

PART TWO

IMPLEMENTATION STRATEGIES

—■—

TRANSFER TO AN INDEPENDENT INSTITUTION

PROGRAM DESCRIPTIONS

CONCLUSION

The independent college or university that commits itself to facilitating transfer recognizes transfer as an opportunity, not a problem. Transfer affords the independent institution multiple opportunities:

☐ to attract additional students
☐ to diversify its collegiate population
☐ to establish closer relations with neighboring institutions
☐ to increase public goodwill.

Of course, a primary reward is an enrollment increase. Independent institutions have difficulty competing for students against neighboring four-year public colleges, no matter how aggressively they keep costs down. Some students who attend low- or no-tuition two-year colleges, however, may have sufficient resources to afford two years at an independent institution. More important, a reputation for facilitating transfer encourages more high school students to plan for transfer. In a competitive environment, fewer independent schools can neglect students who often transfer—by default—to public institutions. Independent institutions that traditionally attract transfer students from other four-year colleges are particularly well-positioned to encourage transfer of two-year college students.

Many independent institutions will benefit by recruiting from the heterogeneous student bodies found in

The most successful institutions
viewed their participation in AAC's project
as part of a comprehensive effort
to remove all transfer barriers

two-year colleges. Admission of older and minority students helps diversify the composition of four-year schools, thereby enriching the experience of all students. Facilitating transfer may help to reduce interinstitutional competition for first-year students and may stimulate other forms of cooperation. Such cooperation improves good will and makes institutions more attractive to external agencies and benefactors that promote further innovation.

Transfer from a public two-year college to an independent four-year college or university can be difficult to regularize. Independent institutions feel less compulsion to work with other institutions than do public four-year colleges. Consortial agreements, when they exist, usually are with other independent, four-year schools. Academic calendars may not resemble those of institutions just down the road, and independent colleges and universities rarely will modify their calendars in deference to nearby public institutions.

One hopeful exception was a spring 1988 switch by Northern Virginia's community college system and Virginia Tech from a quarter to a semester system. This move placed them on the same academic calendar with the state's other public higher-education institutions. "It will help us because many of our students transfer to four-year institutions, most of which are on semesters," notes Barbara Wyles, Northern Virginia Community College associate dean for curricular services.

The higher tuition charged by most independent colleges and universities is in itself a major barrier to transfer. Most students find it difficult to go from a free or nearly free community college to a high-tuition private institution. According to the final report of Kalamazoo College, a participant in the AAC/Mellon project:

It is more convenient and less expensive for a KVCC [Kalamazoo Valley Community College] student to complete a bachelor's degree at Western Michigan University or Nazareth College than at Kalamazoo College. Hence, most of them choose to do so. Relative to other institutions in our market, Kalamazoo College is very expensive. While the majority of our student body receives some form of financial assistance, it is difficult to convince a two-year student—who often is uninformed of the financial aid process—that he or she can afford the cost of a private education. Once students express interest in Kalamazoo, we inundate them with information about financial aid, but we fear our price tag functions in the same way as our reputation—students dismiss us as prohibitively expensive before they even inquire about the possibilities for help.

Few institutions reduce tuition charges for transfer students since that might affect the direct flow of high school graduates into their institutions. A few colleges and universities, including Kalamazoo, offer scholarships for transfer students, but the amounts may not be enough to overcome the competitive advantage of the public colleges. Here we can only note the existence of financial aid barriers and the need for financial aid counseling at the community colleges and the secondary schools. The AAC/Mellon project did not allocate funds for increased scholarship aid, though Mellon provides funding to some institutions.

Many independent colleges and universities have either neglected or rejected efforts to facilitate transfer. Some institutions may have refrained from making commitments to facilitating transfer that required major investments of time, energy, and human and financial resources. Independent college administrators need to match the requisite investments to the potential rewards. The previous chapter of this handbook offered criteria by which to determine whether a major commitment to transfer is appropriate. The salutary results reported by the pilot independent institutions in the AAC/

Mellon Transfer Project lead us to conclude that many independent colleges and universities should place additional resources into facilitating transfer.

PROGRAM DESCRIPTIONS

The following case studies demonstrate how independent institutions with differing levels of experience facilitated transfer. Some schools, such as Kalamazoo, had not thought seriously about transfer until their selection for the AAC/Mellon project. These institutions usually emphasized removal of one set of transfer barriers: recruitment, faculty interaction, or curriculum, for example. Schools with some experience built on their strengths or removed barriers that they could not previously address. The most successful institutions viewed their participation in the AAC/Mellon Transfer Project as part of a comprehensive effort to remove all transfer barriers. Indeed, the institutions with the most experience took steps to assure that the eliminated barriers to transfer remained removed. These schools became examples for other institutions to emulate.

Our project descriptions and comments begin with the preliminary efforts and move to the complicated and advanced projects. We hope that other independent four-year institutions (as well as potential two-year college partners) will use these accounts to help evaluate the benefits and costs of facilitating transfer.

KALAMAZOO COLLEGE

Partner: Kalamazoo Valley Community College

Kalamazoo College (KC) had little experience with two-year transfer before its participation in the AAC/Mellon project. It began a project that emphasized recruitment by preparing a publication for potential transfer students. Such booklets also clarify the aspects of transfer that the four-year institution must address to assure a viable effort. KC addressed the initial booklet to all possible transfer students, from four-year as well as two-year schools. The college then added a brief insert on community college transfer. Experience at other institutions shows that booklets aimed directly at the two-year college student maximize the perception of serious intention.

KC undertook other steps that experts on transfer frequently recommend. KC invited Kalamazoo Valley Community College (KVCC) faculty members to visit its campus. Such visits raise the consciousness of two-year college faculty members about the four-year institution as a possible recipient of their students. They also increase contacts between two- and four-year college faculty members that are crucial for reducing faculty concerns about quality. KC issued the invitation, however, at a time when KVCC was not in session. The disappointing turnout alerted KC to the importance of calendar issues.

KC also agreed to perform a preliminary credit evaluation within two weeks after accepting any KVCC student; before their agreement, KC had waited until just prior to the beginning of the fall quarter. Other initial steps that KC took included staff visits to KVCC, improved data collection concerning transfer students, and production of materials for use by KVCC faculty and staff members in counseling.

Independent colleges and universities with little or no experience with transfer can begin with similar activities. These efforts can be routinized and updated as needed with minimal cost or effort.

OCCIDENTAL COLLEGE

Partners: Glendale Community College and Pasadena City College

Occidental College (Oxy), though enrolling a significant number of transfer students each year, matriculated few students from its nearby two-year college partners: Glendale Community College (GCC) and Pasadena City College (PCC). Although about 350 GCC students transfer annually, in 1985 only six went to Oxy. Oxy's internal evaluation listed familiar barriers: uncertainty about how to reach transfer students, misconceptions about and limited amounts of financial aid, and insufficient transfers of credit. To make matters worse, an extensive and inexpensive public college system was nearby.

The AAC/Mellon grant resulted in slow progress during the first year. Oxy delegated the main responsibility for administering the AAC/Mellon grant to an overburdened admissions office staff member. The initial proposal for improving transfer centered on "passive" activities: encouraging counseling staff and faculty members to work together, giving admissions literature and recommendation forms to PCC and GCC counselors and faculty members, having Oxy transfer students call or write potential transfer students at PCC and GCC, developing brochures for transfer students, and revising the Oxy application form to take the needs and experiences of transfer students into account.

None of these ideas was "wrong," but experience elsewhere shows that such steps are not sufficiently comprehensive. Placing the entire project in the hands of one individual was a bad omen. Worse, the initial Oxy agenda lacked "active" undertakings: for example, having qualified two-year college students visit the Oxy campus, having student transfers return to the two-year college to give advice and information, and having the grant director—admittedly overburdened—visit the partner colleges.

Oxy soon undertook a midcourse correction. Its officials arranged meetings with their administrative counterparts at GCC and PCC, developed ties between corresponding academic departments, arranged for Oxy faculty members to lecture at PCC and GCC, and produced basic publications on transfer. In addition, Oxy obtained a separate grant to hire two-year college students as summer research assistants for Occidental faculty members.

The relationship between Occidental College and its partners gained full momentum after their presidents met. The two-year college presidents confirmed that Oxy officials were speaking to counterparts with authority in their respective areas (a condition not always clear to Oxy officials). They suggested that Oxy

☐ designate PCC and GCC as "redirect institutions," where able but insufficiently prepared Oxy applicants might study for a year before transferring (The students would fulfill specific requirements.)

☐ inform students, faculty members, and counselors of its financial aid plans

☐ prepare a list of its faculty members who would offer guest lectures

☐ give special attention to students designated "honors at entrance" by the community colleges

The pace of interaction accelerated. By the end of the year, twelve PCC and GCC counselors visited Occidental and met admissions staff and faculty members; nine GCC faculty members met with Oxy counterparts, and plans for a formal articulation agreement with PCC emerged. Oxy virtually concluded the PCC agreement during the following academic year, and it signed an agreement with GCC. An Oxy intern informed two-year college students about opportunities at Occidental and later reviewed applications of students she had counseled. Academic division chairs from the partner schools designed programs to help transfer students prepare for their chosen major. At a meeting with Oxy officials, current students who had transferred from two-year colleges voiced concerns about financial aid. These students stressed the importance of singling out the off-campus working transfer student for special attention. The presence of Occidental alumni in key positions at PCC and GCC facilitated the success of some initiatives.

Soon after, GCC invited Occidental President Richard C. Gilman to speak at its commencement. The move both ratified and advanced the relationship between the institutions. These steps did not result in an immediate increase in Oxy's "yield." President Gilman instead cited the opening of lines of communication as the most productive and promising outcome of the grant. A successful program, Oxy learned, requires not only presidential commitment but also patience.

As the AAC/Mellon grant ended, Occidental planned to send an intern back to the two-year colleges to clarify its articulation agreement with GCC with respect to Oxy's core requirement and to expand an information sheet into a handbook for potential transfers. Previously a college with little experience with transfer, Occidental now was ready to make permanent the gains that resulted from participation in the AAC/Mellon project.

KNOX COLLEGE

Partners: Carl Sandburg Community College, Illinois Central Community College, Black Hawk East Community College, and William Rainey Harper College

Knox College had a long-standing but loose articulation agreement with its neighbor, Carl Sandburg Community College (CSCC), about four miles away. Under the agreement, Knox awarded two years of credit to any CSCC student who transferred with a completed A.A. or A.S. degree. Knox also earmarked a scholarship for highly qualified CSCC transfer students. Aside from these measures, Knox had little experience in transfer.

Knox hired a former community college president as project consultant who initiated dialogues first with CSCC and Illinois Central Community College (ICCC), then with Black Hawk Community College (BHCC) and William Rainey

Harper College (WRHC) in suburban Chicago. Its modest initiatives included

☐ development of student transfer planning workbooks. These workbooks used institution-specific information, including course equivalents, to design a course of study, assess the probability of transfer admission, estimate transfer credit and course placement, estimate financial aid eligibility, and assess extracurricular opportunities.

☐ early identification of potential transfer students. The presence of Knox alumni on the CSCC faculty facilitated identification of prospects and interinstitutional discussions.

The discussions produced other suggestions: more exposure while students are still at the two-year college to the kinds of assignments they will receive at the four-year institution; increased four-year counseling support for transfer students; possible joint admissions programs; faculty and student staff exchanges and interactions; and the use of transfer students as recruiters.

Knox officials soon concluded that a successful transfer program required a more comprehensive approach that emphasized the removal of financial barriers. Faculty recommendations could identify potential transfers, but these students had to be convinced through direct approaches that a Knox education was within financial reach. While a Knox education cost more than $11,000 per year, tuition at partner two-year colleges was as low as $22 per credit.

Financial aid counselors would visit the two-year colleges to discuss candidly how students could meet costs. They would explain that most students incur debt, and they would discuss the many financial programs available. They hoped to convince potential transfer students that a liberal education at a small residential college would be a good economic investment.

Knox produced a financial aid brochure that argued that education at an independent college is affordable and that transfer students are treated equally. Knox encouraged potential transfer students to apply for both admission and aid; Knox officials believed that many students did not apply for aid because of low tuition at two-year colleges.

Knox staff members then returned to the issue of course transfers. Knox's partners argued that an articulation agreement that granted junior status but did not guarantee transferability of required general-education and major courses would not remove the major barriers to transfer. The partners asked Knox to guarantee that specified courses would count toward the B.A. and the major and assure junior status. Knox faculty members met with

counterparts at the two-year colleges to formulate lists of equivalencies. These meetings culminated in an articulation agreement with ICCC. Later, Knox issued a draft list of ICCC courses (and their Knox equivalents) that it would accept. The list noted that most courses would count toward the major requirement.

These agreements and course lists required Knox to reflect carefully upon its academic mission and its specific offerings. They helped Knox build a more comprehensive relationship with its partners by establishing standards. These standards could be improved upon; they were difficult to ignore. By addressing the two most difficult barriers to transfer, Knox was on its way toward a comprehensive approach to facilitating transfer.

CLARK COLLEGE

Partners: Atlanta Junior College, Georgia; Broward Community College, Florida; Chabot Community College, California; DeKalb Community College, Georgia; LaGuardia Community College, New York; Miami-Dade Community College, Florida; and Valencia Community College, Florida

Although previously not active in transfer facilitation, Clark College—a historically black, coeducational, independent institution—undertook a geographically broad-based effort. Observers generally applauded its efforts.

Clark prides itself on its liberal arts orientation and its attractiveness to students from low-income families. Although Clark keeps tuition low, more than 90 percent of its students require financial aid. Before it took part in the AAC/Mellon project, 85 percent of Clark's one hundred annual transfers came from other four-year colleges. Clark identified several barriers to transfer: tuition and fee charges, nonacceptance of the D grade, and nontransferability of certain courses.

Clark officials believed that enhancing transfer from two-year colleges would be a hedge against freshman enrollment decreases and student attrition. They also believed that articulation agreements with urban two-year colleges offered an opportunity to minority students who otherwise would have terminated their education. Clark identified five urban institutions: Atlanta Junior College (AJC), Broward Community College (BCC), DeKalb Community College (DCC), LaGuardia Community College (LCC), and Miami-Dade Community College (MDCC).

Clark emphasized the importance of personal contacts at each of the partner institutions. For example, a staff member at BCC was a Clark alumnus and trustee. Clark alumni also were counselors and deans at Valencia Community College (VCC), LCC, and AJC. Prior to the AAC/Mellon project, the Broward staff member facilitated a "two-plus-two" agreement with Clark. The agreement provided that BCC would waive fees for recommended black students in the upper 25 percent of their high school graduating classes with a GPA of 3.0 or higher. Clark offered participating recipients of the Broward associate degree junior status and a scholarship covering tuition and fees. Aid from both colleges continued as long as the student maintained a 3.0 average.

At the outset of the AAC/Mellon project, Clark's president assured his key administrators of his enthusiastic support for facilitating transfer. Clark's negotiating team included the dean of admissions, the chair of the counseling department, the veterans' adviser, the director of cooperative learning, and the registrar.

Clark's participation in the Atlanta University Center (AUC) and its unique relationship with AJC offset its inexperience with two-year college transfer. AUC included three other undergraduate institutions, two graduate schools, and a medical school. All member institutions automatically recognized coursework completed at another member school. Clark and AJC faculty members and students often met informally and frequently conducted course and teacher exchanges. The interaction that other AAC/Mellon project participants tried to encourage already existed between Clark and AJC faculty members. Faculty members visited each others' classrooms to understand the academic demands made upon students and to break down the suspicion of four-year instructors about the quality of two-year college offerings. Clark had no summer school, but many of its students already attended the AJC summer session. Students routinely transferred equivalent courses. Clark offered a final reason for its commitment: "Our commitment as an institution historically has been to take students where they are academically and prepare them for the larger society; hence lengthy 'academic elitist' conversations are minimized."

Broward, a predominantly white community college, raised funds from churches, black fraternities, and other sources to subsidize black attendance. The college extensively advertised its two-plus-two agreement with Clark and emphasized that minority high school students could attend the Broward/Clark program essentially for free. Broward then implemented other programs

to motivate high school and middle school students to attend college. The relationship between Broward and Clark continues to grow. Student groups frequently visit the partner campus. The same Broward staff member who initiated the two-plus-two agreement arranged for the Clark trustees to meet at Broward. Broward then used the leverage that the agreement provided to negotiate similar agreements with nearby Florida A&M University and Bethune-Cookman College. (Florida A&M placed a final cap on the number of students admitted on this basis; others did not.)

Clark's articulation agreement states that it awards transfer credit for all academic courses taken for credit in baccalaureate and associate degree programs at accredited institutions. The content of such courses has to be equivalent to courses offered at Clark. When no parallel exists, Clark makes individual decisions. Only courses for which there is a Clark equivalent course, however, meet requirements for the major.

Clark admits with junior standing any student with a liberal arts associate degree from a two-year college with which it has an articulation agreement, so long as the student completes sixty semester hours or ninety quarter hours—both the minimum and the maximum number—of transferable credits. Clark awards course credit only when a student receives a grade of C or better.

By 1987, seven two-year colleges had entered into articulation agreements with Clark. As the AAC/Mellon project drew to a close, Clark initiated similar discussions with still other community colleges, including Lawson State Community College in Birmingham, Alabama, and Cuyahoga Community College in Cleveland, Ohio.

Clark and AJC officials had concluded that the expectations for student skills and abilities had to be virtually identical for meaningful articulation to occur. This conclusion led to curricular changes and course adjustments. AJC, for example, changed its introductory business and accounting courses to meet the specifications of similar courses at Clark. AJC also intensified its counseling system. Advisers discussed every Clark course requirement, as well as nonacademic aspects of life at Clark. The physical distance between Clark and several partners prompted Clark officials to develop printed materials about the school's environment, personnel, faculty, living conditions, social milieu, and employment opportunities. Clark officials could not assume that all potential transfer students had either the finances or the time to visit the campus.

The educator of many black students who have gone on to administrative and faculty positions throughout the South, and indeed the nation, Clark is in a unique position to establish a national network of feeder two-year colleges. Its officials deemed such personal contacts essential for a successful transfer program. "I realize that credit transfers and faculty acceptance are important," wrote one Clark official, "but people with the appropriate attitudes will make the positive difference.... People make programs successful, while guidelines assist in their governance."

Counterparts at AJC echoed this sentiment. One official testified that the long-standing friendships between the presidents of Clark and AJC, and between himself and his Clark counterpart, along with presidential support (the presidents regularly visited each other's institutions), were the two prerequisites for a successful program. While other initiatives within the AAC/Mellon project demonstrate that such relationships may not always be *sufficient* for success, Clark's program shows that in most cases, they are *necessary*. Moreover, Clark's strategy demonstrates that continued cultivation of alumni bodes well for the institutionalization of reform.

JACKSONVILLE UNIVERSITY

Partner: Florida Community College–Jacksonville

Jacksonville University (JU) had some experience with two-year college transfer before its participation in the AAC/Mellon project. Its officials determined that an emphasis on recruitment from two-year colleges was important for maintaining its enrollment levels. JU worked with the two campuses of Florida Community College–Jacksonville (FCCJ) that stressed liberal academic offerings.

JU's activities centered around recruitment of students who already were inclined toward transfer and had completed most of their FCCJ studies. Its most notable activities included a page in the FCCJ catalogue that offered general information for FCCJ students considering transfer to Jacksonville, joint meetings of student honor societies and other student organizations, and an FCCJ open house on the JU campus to which all graduating FCCJ students received personal invitations. Jacksonville emphasized informal sym-

bolic communication such as the personalized student invitation and hand delivery of a new transfer handbook to an FCCJ official as well as substantive initiatives such as joint administrative exchange luncheons attended by the institutions' presidents. In contrast to other AAC/Mellon project colleges, such as Kalamazoo, JU aimed its transfer brochure specifically at the partner institution. JU also published a handbook that listed every major, the course requirements for each, and the corresponding courses offered at FCCJ.

The project's initial successes led to negotiation of a full-scale articulation agreement in 1986–87. The key points of the agreement included

☐ use of the state college articulation agreement as a model

☐ recognition, full acceptance, and transfer of the FCCJ general-education core and up to sixty-four credit hours for students with the A.A. degree and limited access to special JU programs

☐ creation of an FCCJ/JU Articulation Committee chaired by the respective vice presidents. The JU representatives included deans and faculty representatives.

☐ a clear understanding that students must have completed the A.A. and passed all College Level Academic Skills Test subtests

☐ a revised JU page in the FCCJ

catalogue that discussed the articulation agreement and the special programs available at JU

☐ JU financial aid reserved for FCCJ students

☐ prior notification of proposed curricular changes to allow the partner institution to comment before action is taken

☐ identification of "non-acceptable" courses (as is done in state articulation agreements).

JU's experience shows how programs can become both more comprehensive and more institutionalized. Indeed, throughout the project, the institutions at which informal agreements led to formal agreements were most successful in enhancing transfer. Jacksonville's experience demonstrates that increased formality does not necessarily imply the elimination of the spirit behind the agreements.

UNIVERSITY OF PUGET SOUND

Partners: Tacoma Community College and Pierce Community College

The University of Puget Sound (UPS) used the AAC/Mellon grant to increase its enrollment of minority transfer students. UPS planned to intervene early in the careers of black two-year college business administration majors and facilitate their admission to UPS.

In 1985, UPS enrolled about 400 transfer students, including 220 from community colleges. Before receiving the AAC/Mellon grant, UPS had entered into transfer agreements with all of Washington's community colleges. The agreements provided for guaranteed junior standing for liberal arts transfer students with at least seventy-five quarter hours of transferable credit. Students who took equivalent courses at the community colleges could complete all but one of UPS's general-education requirements. The transfer process itself was carefully administered. An external adviser noted:

> The University maintains up-to-date transfer sheets and articulation recommendations. An advising manual is readily available, and the university's core requirements are clearly stated. Course equivalents are clearly spelled out. Students can transfer ten of the eleven courses listed in the lower division core, and most students who do transfer have completed most of these course requirements, enabling them to enter as juniors. Furthermore, the university will accept up to ninety-six quarters

Success in minority transfer
is not automatic
even for colleges experienced in transfer

earned by transferring students.

The transfer statistics, though sizable (especially for a high-tuition independent institution), represented a 10 percent decline in only two years. Rather than redouble their efforts to attract liberal arts students—approximately fifty per year already transferred from nearby Tacoma Community College (TCC)—UPS used the AAC/Mellon grant to target black business administration majors and potential majors. TCC's proximity and its history of successful transfer with UPS boded well for the project. UPS assumed that most transfers would matriculate in its School of Business and Public Administration. It followed some now-familiar strategies. The respective presidents agreed to support the venture, and the institutions created a schedule to identify, prepare, and assess potential transfer students. UPS established a comprehensive program: Transfer candidates would receive academic, social, and financial counseling; visit UPS; and meet with current faculty members and transfer students.

Notwithstanding UPS's track record on transfer and the clear focus of the AAC/Mellon transfer initiative, these efforts resulted in no additional transfer students. The reasons are instructive.

☐ *Academic factors.* The average GPA of community college transfer students to UPS was 3.01; seventeen of the thirty-one students identified as candidates for transfer had GPAs of less than 2.49. Project officials decided to include students with GPAs less than the usual 2.0, but stipulated that the deficiencies would have to be in areas where the UPS Study Skills Center could help and that a student's participation in the program would not involve a promise of admission. Of the thirty-one students contacted, only five appeared for initial counseling and only two appeared for preliminary testing. One of the identified students already had been rejected for transfer admission. By the end of the academic year, none of the identified students was still participating in the transfer program.

☐ *Social factors.* Investigation by a black UPS student revealed academic and social factors that inhibited participation. Black students expressed a general apathy toward higher education and questioned its ultimate "payoff." They resisted the prospect of transferring to an "all-white, upper middle class" institution. Indeed, of twenty-eight hundred graduates in the UPS class of 1985, about forty were black. Black students said the UPS social and cultural programs were inadequate. They also felt ill-prepared for the rigors of the UPS program and feared failure at a prestigious school.

☐ *Cost of education.* UPS's tuition

was about $6,000 more than TCC's. Nearby Pacific Lutheran University offered more lucrative scholarships.

UPS officials proposed several measures for increasing the minority cohort from which the college might select transfers. UPS added Pierce Community College (PCC)—another proximate community college with a sizable minority constituency—to the program. PCC already sent twice as many minority student transfers to UPS as TCC. UPS redesigned its printed materials on transfer by adapting a successful brochure designed by the University of Arizona under an AAC/Mellon grant. UPS expanded the recruitment pool to include liberal education students as well as business majors. UPS asked TCC transfer students to serve as recruiters and involved the UPS Black Student Union.

The university also increased faculty involvement (which was minimal during the first year) and targeted other minority groups. "The essential actions, then," wrote a consultant, "are to broaden the definition of 'potential transfer,' phone members of that cohort to encourage them to come to meetings, have a group of UPS and TCC representatives meet with the students, pair the students with temporary big brothers and big sisters for campus visits, and thus make it more likely that a group of at least twelve or fif-

teen students would transfer."

UPS, a four-year college with a good record in overcoming transfer barriers, thus drastically changed the focus of its AAC/Mellon project. This experience demonstrates the importance of asking the proper threshold questions before embarking on a major effort. A well-developed relationship led UPS to look to TCC as a partner. Despite its large enrollment, TCC graduated only about two hundred students each year, and many of these students already went to UPS. Furthermore, TCC already had several transfer programs aimed at minorities, including quarterly "Transfer Day," annual transfer workshops, and tours of four-year colleges. This "ceiling effect," combined with the small black enrollment at UPS, boded ill for immediate success.

Our recommendations in Chapter Three include the questions that must be asked before a college invests its resources in a transfer project. Success in minority transfer is not automatic even for colleges experienced in transfer. If an institution wishes to increase its proportion of minority students, a general improvement of transfer conditions is probably insufficient. As UPS's experience shows, moreover, even targeted efforts do not always pay off.

UNIVERSITY OF MIAMI

Partners: Miami-Dade Community College and Broward Community College

The University of Miami (UM) wished to create a university-wide articulation agreement with its AAC/Mellon project partners: Miami-Dade Community College (MDCC) and Broward Community College (BCC). UM admitted upwards of seven hundred transfer students per year, and as many as four hundred came from MDCC. MDCC sent a large proportion of its degree recipients to four-year institutions. A survey conducted in the early 1980s showed that 39 to 49 percent of MDCC associate of arts degree recipients and 10 percent of its associate of science graduates typically continued their education after one year. The number of MDCC students receiving the A.A. degree, however, substantially declined in the mid-1980s when the college imposed higher graduation standards (including the College Level Academic Skills Test required of all Florida A.A. candidates). Most students at Broward Community College (BCC)

in Fort Lauderdale (about sixty miles north) were in the transfer track, and about 60 to 65 percent actually transferred. While MDCC is largely (about 70 percent) populated by minority students, more than 90 percent of BCC students are white.

An independent university with a strategic plan that called for increased selectivity, UM did not expect great numbers of transfers to result from the project. Instead, it hoped that improved articulation would convince the most qualified community college students to consider attending UM instead of automatically turning to Florida International University, a public college with much lower tuition and attractive transfer arrangements, including participation in a statewide articulation compact. In short, rising academic standards led UM officials to examine whether facilitating transfer might reverse recent declines.

Articulation agreements between MDCC and several of UM's undergraduate colleges—including engineering, business, and arts and sciences—had existed for as long as ten years. Prior to the AAC/Mellon project, the agreements were independent of each other and occasionally contradictory. Many MDCC graduates who entered the arts and sciences college found that some of their general-education credits were disallowed or devalued. UM intended to expand the individual agreements into a university-wide articulation agreement under which it would accept transfers with junior status. This goal involved bringing about articulation agreements in schools that did not have them—communications, nursing, and music—and removing inconsistencies among the extant agreements. UM worked with BCC faculty and staff members to create articulation agreements for business administration and computer science students as models for future efforts.

UM officials arranged a dozen meetings among corresponding administrators and faculty members in similar disciplines at the three institutions to discuss barriers and develop options for their removal. These meetings addressed course content, prerequisites, and sequences.

This project could not have been undertaken by schools less experienced in transfer. What Miami had learned later became apparent to other participants in the AAC/ Mellon project:

☐ Involvement of the presidents and chief academic officers of the participating institutions is essential.

☐ Central ongoing authority must be given to a top campus administrator rather than a subordinate official.

☐ The project must be undertaken in a comprehensive manner. At Miami, the project's coordinator suc-

cessfully marshalled the necessary actors.

☐ The faculty's central role in the articulation effort must be recognized and utilized.

The final agreement was brief and general. A separate exchange of letters spelled out exceptions and qualifications.[4] The key provisions stipulated that for MDCC graduates admitted while the agreement was in force UM would

☐ accord the students junior standing, with the understanding that some students might need to complete prerequisite work for the programs in which they enroll

☐ accept the thirty-six required general-education credits earned at MDCC, including credit for the interdisciplinary core curriculum. These credits would be applied toward the equivalent lower-division general-education requirements of UM's schools and colleges. The thirty-six credits were a minimum; most students would receive more credits toward Miami's sixty-three credit general-education requirement.

MDCC's four required interdisciplinary core courses were the main obstacle to the university-wide agreement. These courses had no UM equivalent, and UM faculty members hesitated to accept them for credit. When informal and committee discussions failed to resolve the issue, it was referred to the Miami

The faculty's central role in the articulation effort must be recognized and utilized

Faculty Council of the College of Arts and Sciences. The council accepted the core credits for a trial period of four years, during which both institutions would monitor the academic records of transfer students.

UM's associate provost demonstrated that MDCC and BCC graduates performed significantly better in UM's junior and senior classes than the average UM student accepted as a freshman. An AAC/Mellon project consultant helped convince UM faculty members that many community college transfers were not primarily interested in vocational education as they often were stereotyped.

The presidents of Miami and MDCC signed the completed agreement in an April 1986 ceremony. Student newspapers and the local Miami media gave the agreement wide publicity. Soon after, UM officials sent all MDCC degree candidates invitations to attend a Transfer Day at which they discussed the agreement's provisions.

UM created a position for a transfer admissions specialist who coordinated a recruitment program that focused on MDCC's campuses. UM officials invited MDCC administrators and advisers to Miami for annual meetings. Finally, Miami published a brochure that listed major requirements and course equivalencies for MDCC transfers.

Ongoing consultation helped the institutions resolve subsequent technical problems and facilitated MDCC's pledge to inform all students about UM's required and recommended courses for programs and majors. Students then could more easily select MDCC electives that UM accepted toward specific program or major requirements. UM and MDCC officials agreed to work toward UM's full acceptance of the sixty credits earned at MDCC as program or major requirements rather than as "free" electives. The agreement's limited duration forced UM and MDCC officials to monitor the program carefully and engage in constant dialogue.

Ongoing presidential direction of the agreement, high-level administrative and faculty participation, and publicity and publications helped assure the project's success. While few four-year institutions can afford the luxury of a full-time transfer admissions specialist, at UM this official helped resolve problems that inevitably emerged.

MDCC derived important benefits from the project. The articulation agreement was a model for agreements with four other nearby, independent four-year institutions. Transfer counseling both improved and increased. Faculty members could reflect on how their offerings articulated with the subjects students would encounter next.

BCC, which had a more tangential relationship with Miami, also reported salutary results. Students with forty-five or more credits were encouraged to obtain counseling that included specific information about Miami. BCC also restructured specific courses, including business calculus, to bring them more in line with UM's offerings. BCC discussed articulation with UM officials in divisions where no agreements yet existed. In addition, as with MDCC, Broward began negotiations on transfer with other independent colleges and universities.

This project demonstrates how an independent institution's commitment helps assure success. UM's initiative, its track record in transfer, and, in the case of arts and sciences at MDCC, its willingness to experiment with an agreement from which it could easily have backed away signaled a commitment that allowed for good will. Both community college partners reported that UM's enthusiasm and professionalism were crucial for the project's success.

VASSAR COLLEGE

Partners: LaGuardia Community College, Dutchess Community College, Orange Community College, Rockland Community College, Sullivan Community College, and Ulster Community College

Building upon a three-year-old collaborative relationship with LaGuardia Community College (LCC), Vassar College established a comprehensive summer program for potential transfer students who completed their first year at five New York State community colleges. Vassar aimed its program primarily at minority students and appointed its adviser to minority students as project director. Its officials believed that the partner colleges enrolled minority students who could adjust to study and social life at a selective residential college. The officials wished to demonstrate to these students that admission to and successful completion of a degree program were realistic goals.

The key barrier for students, Vassar staff members concluded, was not academic, social, or financial but the belief that schools like Vassar were "not for them." Vassar's dean of studies succinctly stated the goal:

> To offer capable and motivated community college students without previous exposure to it a genuine introduction to the selective, residential, liberal arts college experience, and to provide them with the particular supports necessary for their success and for their evaluation of the experience.

LCC's urban (mainly minority) students may have considered transfer to New York City's extensive City University system, but they probably would not have considered Vassar.

The project directors designed a comprehensive program to give potential transfer students an understanding of academic, social, and residential life at a selective college. Vassar offered a five-week residential summer study institute to twenty-six potential transfer candidates. Students who had completed one year of community college work at a partner institution were eligible for admission. Institute faculty members, including instructors at Vassar and the two-year college partners, chose the participants. Students and peer counselors (themselves transfer students) lived together in a dorm in the middle of the Vassar campus. Support personnel included a writing specialist from the academic resource center, a specialist in general study skills, a specialist from the mi-

crocomputer center, and admissions and financial aid advisers.

Faculty and staff members at the two-year colleges helped plan and implement the program and then helped design and coteach the courses offered to admitted students. These introductory courses included "The Science and Practice of Thinking" (cognitive science), "Conflict and Celebration in American Writing" and "Literature and Politics" (literature), "Computing as a Resource" (computer science), "Community Studies" (urban studies), and "Environmental Impacts: Technology, Resources, and Social Values" and "Biology and Ethics: Genetic Engineering" (interdepartmental). The courses had the same range and scope as regular Vassar offerings. Each student took two of three offered courses and received seven or eight academic credits that were routinely accepted by the partner two-year college. Students paid no tuition, though Vassar attempted to recover state and federal funds to which students were entitled.

The spirit of cooperation manifest in the relationships between faculty members carried over to the students. Students initially expressed concern about living away from home and being in the constant company of their peers, but within a few days they formed collaborative study groups. A student peer counselor noted, "Student-instructed mini-classes became...their mode of communication.... Soon, conversations resembled a teaching session and then they resembled a learning experience. There never seemed to be a moment where the students were not learning about academics or about life."[5]

Student collaboration (in addition, of course, to institutional support) helped participants adjust to Vassar's more demanding academic environment and its different social environment. Course grades ranged from A to C+, slightly higher than a typical Vassar course grade range. Student successes in adjusting to these demands helped convince two-year college faculty participants that many of their students were capable of considerable accomplishments. Higher faculty expectations, most assumed, would reduce the gap between student performance in two- and four-year college environments.

This full-time summer program made transfer a central institutional activity, not an additional project for already overburdened two- or four-year college administrators, faculty members, and students. The program demonstrates the importance of commitment and comprehensive planning. The presidents of each participating institution made personal, financial, and institutional commitments that allowed the program to deal successfully with the academic, social, residential, and financial needs of students.

The institute showed that able two-year college students who commit themselves full time to academic inquiry can succeed in a demanding environment. The program's full-time format and its full-cost subsidy allowed participants to spend unusual amounts of "time on task."

Institutional and student commitment translated into good transcripts, heightened self-esteem, and developed abilities. All participants in the first two institutes transferred to four-year colleges—half to public institutions, half to independent institutions. Program officials believed that the students who elected independent colleges would not have done so except for the institute.

With Ford Foundation support in 1988, Vassar and AAC invited a group of selective liberal arts colleges to emulate the Vassar initiative. Vassar's success bodes well for emulation. The two problems that these programs must confront are financial costs and institutionalization. During the 1986 summer institute, thirty-one students received credit for 219 semester hours at a cost of $836 per credit. This amount was less than the cost of a regular Vassar credit, but it was substantially higher than the cost of a credit at any partner two-year college. Since cost factors

The word 'partnership' is not a euphemism for 'imposition'

often are a major barrier to transfer, plans for growth must take this relatively high cost into account.

The need for institutionalization is related to the financial question. The institute was heavily subsidized by foundation funds. Without assurance of program permanence, students could not plan for program participation in advance. Nor would there be room for experimentation. Should the same faculty members repeat their offerings year after year, one memo asked, or should faculty members be rotated to expose more of them to the program? Lacking assurance of permanence, a full range of contacts between two- and four-year partners would not develop.

Vassar emphasized both the importance of the personal element in making its program work and the need for the program's intitutionalization. "Vassar is committed for the foreseeable future to the development and continuation of the summer program for community college students," stated one report. Future plans include improvements in student financial aid arrangements and faculty recruitment and participation of former institute students as recruiters, mentors, and even, perhaps, underwriters.

Currently there is momentum for increased involvement of highly selective institutions in two-year to four-year college transfer. Indeed, the realization that the loss of momentum could end chances for further experiments for at least a decade itself may be a spur to action.

CONCLUSION

An independent college or university that contemplates a transfer initiative ventures into an area filled with opportunity. These schools, however, typically compete rather than cooperate with other institutions, especially in the area of admissions. An independent college or university that competes with a community college for the same first-year students must be careful to cultivate an authentic transfer partnership with that school. Independent institutions also must be aware that two-year colleges may have articulation agreements with public institutions. Such agreements, in addition to their own considered decisions about the curriculum offered to transfer students, must be taken into careful account when entering into discussions. Partnerships evolve; the word "partnership" is not a euphemism for "imposition."

Projects undertaken by independent institutions that are just beginning to work with transfer typically involve clarification of issues (e.g., Kalamazoo's transfer booklet and Knox's financial aid booklet), passive activities (distributing literature instead of active recruitment), the efforts of one or a few individuals, and establishment of informal relationships (often via alumni, faculty members, or even spouses). Projects begun by institutions with more experience in facilitating transfer usually are more complex and build upon early successes in logical and cooperative fashion. This usually means greater formality, since informal networks and agreements often become victims of increased size of the transfer student contingent, turnover among key personnel, and the need for coordination—victims, at times, of their own success.

Many independent institutions that work with public two-year colleges are predominantly liberal arts institutions. Two-year colleges that attempt to help these institutions facilitate transfer often are constrained by their multiple missions and their public status. A four-year liberal arts institution must anticipate objections from two-year college vocational faculty members, for example. Community colleges often venture into partnerships with four-year institutions, but they are under no obligation to do so, and they often enter into these partnerships at some internal cost.

An independent institution must consider what it is willing to accept. Jacksonville's willingness to base its negotiations on the state college articulation agreement provides one model for independent four-year colleges and universities. This practice maximizes the number of potential transfers and makes the independent institution more competitive. Independent colleges and universities that decline this course, however, have other methods to facilitate transfer.

Colleges and universities must decide whether to give up making credit decisions on a case-by-case basis. In the long run, this practice may lead to inconsistencies, both within a department and among departments. Departments whose institutions wish to facilitate transfer may have to yield on making case-by-case decisions in favor of certifying particular courses at partner institutions. Such certification, however, does not imply giving up their ultimate authority. Should partnerships result in a considerable flow of transfer students, departments soon may welcome the respite from making individual decisions—which usually come at a very bad time in the academic calendar. In any case, the AAC/Mellon project demonstrates that early faculty involvement helps to resolve this issue constructively.

Forcing a one-sided plan upon either a reluctant four-year or two-year institution may end cooperative relations for a decade or longer. As the Miami case indicates, a well-conceived, comprehensive plan need not be considered permanent and unalterable. Nor must a plan be implemented all at once. The Vassar example shows that forming a cooperative relationship between faculty members at partner institutions is a good way to begin. Chances for implementation improve as two- and four-year institutions build mutual trust. An independent college or university that understands that it *and* its partner institutions function in a competitive setting, that a commitment to transfer should involve the patient implementation of a comprehensive plan based on increased mutual trust, and that increased enrollment is only one of a number of salutary outcomes usually will find its efforts rewarded.

TRANSFER TO A PUBLIC INSTITUTION

PROGRAM DESCRIPTIONS

CONCLUSION

The enlightened independent college or university views transfer as an opportunity. The public four-year institution should see transfer enhancement as both an opportunity and a responsibility. The AAC/Mellon project demonstrated that public institutions did not have to lose their "distinctiveness" in order to facilitate transfer. Indeed, they nurtured that distinctiveness by identifying and preparing students who might best profit from their strengths in cooperation with partner two-year colleges.

Some public colleges and universities facilitated transfer in response to heightened efforts by private institutions. These public institutions did not take for granted—but often relied on—a constant flow of transfer students. Faculty and staff members at these schools viewed transfer facilitation as a service to students. Students should not have to conform to the needs of institutions; rather, institutions should change in response to the needs of their students.

PROGRAM DESCRIPTIONS

The AAC/Mellon project included four public four-year institutions. Their prior experiences with transfer had taught them that they had no lock on the local transfer constituency simply because long-standing relationships and formal articulation agreements existed. Indeed, several schools experienced declining numbers of transfers and viewed the

AAC/Mellon project as a way of reinvigorating their partnerships.

TEMPLE UNIVERSITY

Partners: Bucks County Community College, Community College of Philadelphia, Delaware County Community College, and Montgomery County Community College

A large public urban university located in a state that had no overall articulation agreement, Temple had been accepting a significant number of transfer students—25 percent of whom studied at one of four Greater Philadelphia community college partners. The largest number of students transferred from the predominantly black Community College of Philadelphia (CCP); the smallest number came from suburban Delaware County Community College (DCCC). The remainder came from suburban Montgomery County Community College (MCCC) and Bucks County Community College (BCCC). Having few formal relationships with these community colleges, Temple used its AAC/Mellon funds to improve communication and articulation with the schools that al-

ready provided such a substantial percentage of its transfer population.

Temple's size and complexity meant that a comprehensive agreement such as that negotiated between the University of Miami and Miami-Dade Community College (see Chapter Four) required a great deal of work. The university enrolled more than thirty thousand students on four campuses, including fifteen thousand undergraduates located in thirteen different colleges. While participating in the AAC/Mellon project, Temple also was considering a university-wide general-education requirement for its own first- and second-year students. Several departments and colleges resisted articulation discussions and the general-education requirement on the grounds of autonomy. Indeed, the tendency of departments at Temple to add courses to the student major adversely affected both initiatives. Students had difficulty transferring all credits earned at the community colleges toward the Temple baccalaureate degree.

Temple aimed its proposal primarily at students already interested in the institution. Among the initial steps were "two-plus-two" plans for specific units of the university, a thorough determination of equivalencies between community college courses and Temple courses, development of informational booklets for transfer students, computerized information about transfer students, and a recruitment videotape for commuter students.

Temple arranged frequent meetings between admissions staffs, regular transfer days at the partner institutions, and allocation of some scholarships specifically for transfer students. The university suggested some retention activities: a special orientation program, training for academic advisers, cooperative research on transfer students, and reexamination of university regulations that might affect transfer students. Finally, Temple proposed some cooperative endeavors: faculty and student visits, cross-teaching, and courses offered on the partners' campuses.

Faculty apathy was a stumbling block in the colleges that had adequate numbers of students. Some colleges required higher mastery levels for admission to a major than the community colleges offered. Technical programs at Temple required mastery of calculus, for example, while community college mathematics courses emphasized algebra. Some joint meetings took place, but Temple faculty members expressed little interest in exchanges or in offering courses at partner campuses. The exception was in English composition, where faculty members at Temple and its partners wanted to establish common composition-scoring criteria. Those favoring a decrease in the barriers to transfer found they had little leverage.

Temple used its AAC/Mellon grant to engage in both short- and long-term planning. Recognizing the extent of existing obstacles to articulation agreements, the university created a program that allowed for small steps at the outset and greater steps with the acquisition of experience. The university did create a list of equivalencies for frequently transferred courses and launched plans for a two-plus-two program in several divisions. Temple hoped that symbolic (e.g., the AAC/Mellon grant) and substantive (the course equivalency list) accomplishments would lead to greater faculty cooperation and reduction of other transfer barriers.

UNIVERSITY OF MASSACHUSETTS-BOSTON

Partners: Roxbury Community College and Bunker Hill Community College

The University of Massachusetts–Boston (UMB) is highly dependent upon transfer students. More than 60 percent of the 1986–87 undergraduate class entered as transfer students from other four-year schools. Between fall 1984 and fall 1985, the number of community college transfer students increased from 377 to 454. Competition from ninety independent colleges and universities within the state as well as thirty-three public institutions—including sixteen community colleges—gave UMB an impetus to facilitate transfer.

Both project partners sent many students to four-year colleges and universities. Most transfers from Roxbury Community College (RCC)—98 percent of whom were from minority groups—went to independent institutions. At Bunker Hill Community College (BHCC), 34 percent of its 445 graduates in 1984 and 34 percent of its 529 graduates in 1985 transferred to four-year institutions, again with many going to independent colleges and universities. Although thirty BHCC students transferred to UMB in 1984, only fourteen did so in 1986. As is true elsewhere, other students transferred without completing the requirements for the associate's degree. UMB's AAC/Mellon project responded to the increasing numbers of transfers and restimulated student interest at schools such as BHCC, whose graduates transferred elsewhere.

UMB faced many constraints. A statewide transfer compact made acceptance easy but, critics argued, forced most students to repeat much of the general-education component. Some observers interpreted state policy to mean that UMB's attempt to raise academic standards took precedence over transfer facilitation. The academic distance between two- and four-year institutions appeared considerable because many individuals on the four-year campus believed that the community colleges accommodated students with marginal academic ability. An AAC/Mellon consultant noted "a strong sense of status differentials" and "considerable complexity and diversity within the system" that affected attitudes toward transfer.

State officials argued that Massachusetts institutions had considerable autonomy and that the state encouraged institutional initiatives. During the period of the AAC/Mellon project, the Massachusetts Board of Regents established a Transfer Coordinating Committee to review, revise, and reactivate the state's Commonwealth Compact Agreement. The regents also set up regional articulation committees to promote better communication among local two- and four-year colleges. UMB and BHCC cohosted a meeting of eastern group deans to launch the initiative.

Prior to the AAC/Mellon project,

UMB had two articulation agreements in place. An agreement with RCC provided for cross-registration and guaranteed slots in UMB's School of Nursing to students who successfully completed a specified program of study. UMB also had an informal agreement in early childhood learning with BHCC and sponsored a scholarship program for community college transfer students. UMB's multifaceted transfer project proposed to

☐ evaluate data on transfer students collected by RCC and BHCC in the early 1980s and conduct follow-up interviews to determine the factors that led to successful transfer. UMB's Office of Planning established the position of assistant to the vice chancellor for planning to monitor progress of transfer students from its partners.

☐ organize a steering committee for orientation and retention that would evaluate existing procedures and suggest improvements

☐ organize meetings among faculty members in departments where UMB officials perceived ambiguities in articulation

☐ establish a model transfer program for potential teachers using the RCC/UMB nursing transfer program as a model.

These were elementary steps for a public institution that nominally participated in a statewide transfer compact. UMB produced new informational brochures, a manual for transfer counselors, and a computerized transfer equivalency guide (the first in the state). Placing the guide on a computer allowed for rapid updating and expedited review of an applicant's credentials. UMB also developed a "two-plus-two" manual with RCC, created new community college visitation programs, and established a new administrative position to coordinate transfer activities. Previously students had complained that communication was absent among various administrative offices at UMB.

UMB's program did not address two major barriers that were noted by outside evaluators.

☐ inconsistent general-education requirements among UMB divisions. Such inconsistencies caused problems because UMB enrolled a high proportion of undeclared majors. Students complained that weak advising complicated matters.

☐ placement and competency policies and exams. Students and faculty members said the placement exams offered to transfer students measured competencies that were not taught in courses that presumably prepared them for the tests. Many transfer students failed the writing proficiency exam or postponed taking it beyond the recommended time.

Once aware of these barriers, UMB

officials shifted priorities and used the remaining AAC/Mellon funds to create a critical thinking and writing course for selected community college transfer students. UMB officials proposed to visit selected community colleges—chosen for their minority populations—and assist advanced students in applying to the university. The university would examine writing proficiency during the semester before matriculation and encourage students who failed the exam to enroll in the critical thinking and writing course to be offered free during each summer. Students who took the course would receive special tutoring and advising during their first semester at UMB.

Direction from the highest echelons was lacking at UMB. Concerned middle-level administrators and faculty members, who should have dealt mainly with policy implementation, often played inappropriate roles. UMB officials assessed the barriers to transfer and established priorities within a comprehensive framework only with great effort. UMB's real accomplishments through the AAC/Mellon grant, however, and its enumeration of future priorities bode well for a change in its image from barrier erector to facilitator.

UNIVERSITY OF ARIZONA

Partners: Pima Community College District and Cochise College

The University of Arizona (UA) is highly dependent upon transfer students. UA defined a transfer student as any student who brought twelve or more units from another institution of higher education. About 40 percent of UA's enrollment met this definition, and about half this number came from community colleges. Nearly 2,600 students enrolled at UA during 1985–86 previously had studied at the three campuses of Pima Community College District (PCCD), also located in Tucson. About eight hundred students transferred each year, and another eight hundred simultaneously enrolled in both institutions. Cochise College, which serves the southeastern part of the state, sent about seventy-five students per year to UA.

UA's commitment to transfer and articulation included the appointment of a special assistant for academic articulation. UA's arts and sciences college and Cochise cooperated in a "two-plus-two" program, one of several articulation agreements that already existed between UA and its partner institutions. Arrangements between UA and PCCD already included a Cooperative Effort Committee that met several times a year, an annual PCCD/UA counselor workshop, a writing-across-the-curriculum project, and an automated course-evaluation project. UA admissions personnel, faculty members, and administrators regularly had visited PCCD campuses. Faculty representatives from the two schools had met annually to hear reports from the presidents and to discuss transfer-related issues.

UA also had participated in statewide articulation efforts. UA's vice president for academic affairs belongs to Arizona's statewide Academic Program Articulation Steering Committee. UA also hosts an annual community college academic officer's conference, conducts advising and preregistration sessions on community college campuses, and sends representatives from its Office of Minority Student Affairs to some community colleges. Finally, UA also participates in statewide articulation efforts that involve Arizona's other four-year colleges. These efforts include participating on statewide committees and task forces and preparing booklets on admissions requirements and course equivalencies.

Thus, UA came to the AAC/

Mellon project with considerable experience with community college transfer students. Other participants in the AAC/Mellon project adopted, for example, its practice of reporting on community college transfer students to the previous institution.

Two-year transfer matriculations at UA had declined steadily, however, while the transfer student dropout rate remained significant. Admission of in-state transfer students fell by 13.9 percent between fall 1984 and fall 1985. In the same period, the number of transfer students admitted from PCCD and Cochise declined from 558 to 504 and from sixty to fifty-five, respectively. The dropout rate was higher for students who transferred with one year of community college work. Students with two years at the community college persisted at the same rate as entering UA first-year students. UA had a sophisticated recruitment apparatus for secondary school students, but it had no similar mechanism for community college students before its participation in the AAC/Mellon project.

UA officials identified five key barriers to transfer:
☐ Inflexible scheduling limited course and degree program offerings in the late afternoons and evenings. A majority of students who participated in the AAC/Mellon project indicated that their work schedules

prevented them from attending day-time courses.

☐ Distance was a major barrier for many Cochise students who lived far from UA and could not relocate.

☐ Inadequate financial aid and financial counseling were major obstacles, especially for minority students. Transfer students, for example, sometimes failed to meet the deadline for applying for aid.

☐ Transfer students feared UA's largeness and associated it with an unfriendly atmosphere.

☐ Transfer students were concerned about UA's rigor and the competitive nature of its environment. "This is probably an accurate perception compared to the more supportive, less competitive environments of some community colleges," one report noted.

UA proposed a comprehensive Higher Education Linkage Plan (HELP) to remove these barriers and thereby improve its transfer services. Two programs lay at the heart of the plan:

☐ UA formalized existing faculty collaborations. Each institution identified faculty members to participate in information exchanges, become familiar with campus facilities and programs, discuss the academic needs of transfer students, and review articulated programs and courses. About two hundred faculty members in fields with the potential for high transfer rates and in skill areas (English and mathematics) attended day-long meetings in which they analyzed baccalaureate programs, articulated specific courses, and developed information for transfer guides. UA hoped that the exchanges might help to upgrade parallel community college courses. The upgraded courses then would reduce the gap between expectations at the two- and four-year levels.

☐ About fifty admissions officers, admissions counselors, financial aid officers, and learning center staff members held similar meetings. They identified a target student population of at least 125 students who would benefit from academic advising and peer mentoring. These students also would visit UA to meet with faculty members, attend classes, and experience orientation.

The community colleges used information from their admissions applications or from enrollment in parallel university programs to supply the names and addresses of potential transfer students. These students received a brochure describing HELP's benefits: early admissions status after satisfactory completion of thirty-six credit hours at the community college, priority registration and housing, dual advising, campus tours, transfer day activities, transcript evaluation, and peer advising. Students who signed up for HELP received a welcome letter that contained specific information about majors, campus services, and dates of admissions officer visits to the community college. Students could call the HELP director or contact people at the UA school to which they intended to transfer.

HELP was not aimed specifically at minority students, but UA encouraged low income, minority, and disabled students to participate. Minority students were referred to the Office of Minority Student Affairs, which offered its own pre- and post-enrollment services. Twenty-two percent of HELP participants were minority students, but UA authorities had expected a higher percentage. This is consistent with findings from the AAC/Mellon project indicating that four-year colleges and universities that were able to increase minority enrollment through community college transfer did so by gearing their programs specifically to the minority constituency. Minority enrollments seem less likely to increase as a by-product of a general program.

The UA proposal addressed nearly every aspect of transfer. Along with the counselor workshops, UA and its partners conducted peer adviser and mentor workshops. Mentors met with potential transfer students who visited UA, and themselves made follow-up visits to the community colleges. Peer

advisers worked with transfer students who had been admitted. UA conducted a special Transfer Day aimed at the students identified through the HELP program. Whereas twelve students had visited UA on Transfer Day the previous year, HELP's administration of the event resulted in 165 visitors. Participants met academic advisers, received assistance with financial aid applications, and toured the UA campus.

UA began plans for an Extended Day Program that would make academic degree programs available after 4 P.M. and on weekends for transfer students unable to attend UA during daytime hours. UA also conducted a workshop for all community college counselors in the state. At the workshop, university officials distributed transfer curriculum guides that included requirements for each university major and the equivalent courses available at the community college.

After transferring to UA, HELP students received special peer transfer assistance to facilitate their adjustment to university life. UA already had been sending its students into the state's high schools to counsel, motivate, and assist potential applicants for admission. The peer program expanded this practice to transfer students. UA also contemplated instituting a summer bridge program that would include other community colleges in the state.

An ambitious, comprehensive plan requires strong support for successful implementation. The presidents of each school met to review and approve every facet of the AAC/Mellon project. Each president identified a liaison and gave that individual access to information and to key individuals.

The HELP program directly addressed several barriers to transfer identified by UA officials. It regularized informal faculty contacts that had resulted from earlier articulation efforts, and it created opportunities for interaction where informal relationships had not existed previously. HELP offered partial tuition waivers for 250 transfer students and full tuition waivers for transfer students accepted into the honors program. The program also reminded students of upcoming deadlines for submitting financial aid applications and sent students step-by-step instructions and application forms.

Students reported that Transfer Day helped break down their concerns about UA's atmosphere and that the Extended Day degree offerings helped address the needs of the 60 percent of HELP students who worked during the day. UA expected that student advising would help convince well-prepared actual and potential transfer students that they could succeed. HELP encourages stu-

dents to remain at the community college until they have completed satisfactorily either thirty-six hours of university-parallel coursework or their lower division courses.

UA did not start its program from scratch. Its experience with articulation and with programs that facilitated access and retention of high school graduates allowed it to build upon a strong base. UA took policies and practices that had existed in one setting and adapted them to others or formalized what previously had been ad hoc and informal. Its comprehensive effort is a model for other programs, especially at public institutions.

CALIFORNIA STATE UNIVERSITY–HAYWARD

Partner: Chabot College

Less than five miles apart, California State University–Hayward (CSUH) and Chabot College already had a strong working relationship. The presidents, chief executive officers, and deans of these two commuter schools met at least once a year to discuss mutual problems. There also were many ties among faculty members; many Chabot faculty members also taught on a part-time basis at CSUH. Between 12 and 20 percent of Chabot faculty members held CSUH degrees. The two schools had a long-standing cross-registration agreement. All of this boded well for the faculty exchanges proposed under the AAC/Mellon grant and for curriculum articulation.

Between 1983 and 1986, about 530 Chabot students transferred each year to the California State University system, and 85 percent of these students went to CSUH. (In contrast, the numbers of students transferring to the University of California system from Chabot were: 1983—seventy-three; 1984—eighty-eight; 1985—seventy-four; 1986—eighty-one.) CSUH had an office of school relations whose staff visited each local community college at least twice a year. CSUH's student affirmative action office worked closely with Chabot administrators to identify and encourage minority students to transfer to a four-year college upon completing the A.A. degree.

Under the AAC/Mellon grant, CSUH proposed to explore seven aspects of its relationship with Chabot:

☐ creation of a Transfer Center at Chabot that would be a constant, visible reminder of the importance of transfer. Identified by a large sign, the center invited students to discuss transfer possibilities. A CSUH official spent one day a week at the center. The center gathered statistics on transfer and facilitated a major academic and demographic study of the students who transferred from Chabot to CSUH.

☐ a survey of current articulation agreements, cross-registration procedures, transfer advising, and student assessment. The two schools used the results of the survey to update all articulation agreements and to plan for continuous updating. CSUH faculty members sometimes changed lower-division major requirements without informing community college counterparts. CSUH amended its curriculum manual to provide for immediate consultation with community colleges about such changes.

☐ use of the A.A. degree as a goal for the transfer student. Chabot's A.A. did not require the completion of the general-education courses needed for transfer to CSUH, and a separate certification was necessary. Chabot had to assess the potential opposition from vocational educators to incorporating general-education transfer requirements into the A.A. program.

☐ a study of minority student transfer. Each campus routinely referred minority students to the other institution when appropriate and pro-

A large public institution with multiple undergraduate divisions poses a special challenge to transfer

vided students with the names of appropriate individuals at the partner institution. The two colleges printed a brochure with pictures of all relevant officials.

☐ an increase in faculty exchanges. Although some part-time faculty members taught at both institutions, there had been only one formal exchange during the previous three years. During the AAC/Mellon project, the colleges arranged new full-quarter, as well as individual, class exchanges.

☐ a study of student interaction, especially through the student associations at each school. Student association presidents suggested exchange visits of student councils and participation in joint celebrations and intramural competition.

☐ a study of financial aid procedures. Some faculty members thought that barriers might result from differences in financial aid programs at the two schools. Areas of difference included amount of funds available and deadlines.

To implement these projects, CSUH and Chabot established a steering committee that included academic senate chairs, admissions officers, counselors, and staff members responsible for minority affairs. The provosts of CSUH and Chabot co-chaired the committee. The top officials of each institution supported the AAC/Mellon project. In fact,

Chabot's key official became that institution's acting president shortly after the project's termination.

The centerpiece of the AAC/Mellon project became the improvement of the associate of arts degree as a transfer vehicle. In 1984–85, only 20 percent of the Chabot transfer students to CSUH had received an A.A. degree. More than 80 percent, however, had completed at least eighty-four quarter units (both colleges operated under the quarter system) of transferable work—nearly the number of credits required for the A.A. degree. More than 70 percent had transfer GPA's of 2.50 or higher. These statistics indicated that most transfer students earned sufficient credit and did work of sufficient quality to receive the associate of arts degree. CSUH did not require an A.A. degree for transfer, however, and the Chabot A.A. did not require courses that met CSUH's general-education requirement. The partners decided to create a degree program that encouraged students to complete the associate of arts program at Chabot and meet CSUH's general-education requirements.

Rather than debate the content of Chabot's current associate of arts degree, Chabot and CSUH officials agreed to create a new Associate of Arts in University Studies (AAUS) degree. Students who obtained this degree with a 2.0 GPA were assured of transfer with junior status to CSUH, as well as to California State University units at Sacramento, San Francisco, and San Jose. The four-year institutions would accept all credits without further credential evaluation.

AAUS degree completion also signified that a student met CSUH's lower-division requirements for general education. (The student still had to complete twelve upper-division units.) AAUS students also had to complete an "area of emphasis" requirement that fulfilled the requirement for a chosen major, either in full or in part, at the four-year school. An area of emphasis consisted of eighteen units in either the social sciences, the natural sciences, or the humanities.

For students who completed a vocational program at Chabot, the Steering Committee agreed to congratulate all degree recipients and inform them that the general-education courses they completed are a start toward a four-year college degree. These students would receive the names of CSUH officials who could advise them further. Officials noted that many minority students took vocational courses and that the largest group of transfer students from Chabot to CSUH majored in business administration (43 percent in 1984–85).

The AAC/Mellon project eased articulation between the two institutions. Chabot worked to develop similar articulation agreements with additional four-year colleges and universities in the state. Other community colleges began to emulate Chabot's innovations, especially the new AAUS program and the Transfer Center. The CSUH-Chabot program proved a model of committed, comprehensive, interinstitutional cooperation.

CONCLUSION

Public four-year colleges and universities have a strong reason to facilitate transfer: the likelihood of immediate and significant enrollment increases. While many independent schools have little or no experience with transfer, some public institutions rely upon transfer students for a considerable proportion of their enrollments. While independent institutions first ask *whether* to facilitate transfer, public colleges and universities first ask *how*. Many independent schools in the AAC/Mellon project received from five to fifteen new transfer students, but most public institutions already had hundreds of two-year transfer students. Public institutions often found that barrier removal brought significant increases or at least ended decreases.

Public colleges and universities, however, cannot assume automatically that they have an advantage over independent institutions when they enter into transfer partnerships with public two-year colleges. The Jacksonville example shows that an aggressive initiative by an independent institution can affect ongoing relationships between public two- and four-year colleges, while the UMB case shows that initiatives undertaken by public institutions are not successful automatically.

A large public institution with multiple undergraduate divisions poses a special challenge to transfer. Two-year colleges may be pulled in different directions by different institutions or by multiple divisions of the same institution. In two of our case studies, conflicting pulls became important when divisions of the same four-year institutions made different determinations about the acceptability of equivalents to their general-education requirements. Coordination among undergraduate units of four-year colleges and universities facilitates transfer and prevents interdivisional competition.

In many states, the statewide articulation agreement is the answer to the multiple conflicting demands made upon two-year colleges. The

AAC/Mellon project, however, found that these agreements often atrophy; in many cases they lack a sound intellectual basis and adequate faculty participation. In the last century, efforts by individual institutions to improve articulation with the high schools led to statewide and then regional accreditation agreements. Similarly, statewide articulation agreements between two- and four-year colleges have the greatest chance for success when they evolve from sound partnerships, such as those in the AAC/Mellon project.

Since World War II, the community college has been in the forefront of plans to increase access to higher education. If the two-year college is to be the first—and not the last—postsecondary institution encountered by the typical high school graduate (and especially the typical minority student), removing barriers to transfer and taking affirmative steps to facilitate the process must be viewed as a national priority. The AAC/Mellon project shows that barriers can be removed and transfer can be facilitated affirmatively. What is needed is commitment to institutionalizing a comprehensive vision.

NOTES

1. See especially Richard C. Richardson, Jr., and Louis W. Bender, *Students in Urban Settings: Achieving the Baccalaureate Degree*, ASHE/ERIC Higher Education Reports 6 (Washington, D.C.: Association for the Study of Higher Education, 1985).

2. D. H. Menke, "A Comparison of Transfer and Native Bachelor's Degree Requirements at UCLA, 1976–78" (Ph.D. dissertation, University of California–Los Angeles, 1980).

3. Arthur M. Cohen et al., *Transfer Education in American Community Colleges* (Los Angeles: Center for the Study of Community Colleges, 1985), chapter 1.

4. These qualifications included waiving the core requirements for some students in selective programs, requiring additional credits in some programs, and validating the work of visual and performing arts students. Extant agreements in engineering, business, and architecture that detailed course requirements and prerequisites remained in force (as more "specific and student protecting"). UM's ongoing relations with MDCC and BCC allowed it to iron out problems in articulation agreements and keep them up to date.

5. For the use of such peer groups as a pedagogical strategy, see Mindy Fullilove, M.D.; Robert E. Fullilove, III; Mark Terris; and Norman Lacayo, "Is Black Achievement an Oxymoron?" *Thought and Action* 4 (Fall 1988): 5–20.

BIBLIOGRAPHY

American Council on Education. *Guidelines for Improving Articulation Between Community, Junior and Senior Colleges.* Washington, D.C.: American Council on Education, 1983.

Astin, Alexander. *Minorities in Higher Education.* San Francisco: Jossey-Bass, 1982.

Bernstein, Allison. "The Devaluation of Transfer: Current Explanations and Possible Causes." In *The Community College and Its Critics*, edited by L. Stephen Zwerling, 31–40. New Directions for Community Colleges Series, no. 54. San Francisco: Jossey-Bass, 1986.

Birnbaum, Robert. "Why Community College Transfer Students Succeed in Four-Year Colleges: The Filter Hypothesis." *Journal of Educational Research* 63 (February 1970): 247–249.

Bogart, Quentin, and Sue I. Murphey. "Articulation in a Changing Higher Education Environment." *Community College Review* 13 (Fall 1985): 17–22.

Boss, Roberta S. "Junior College Articulation: Admission, Retention, Remediation, Transfer." *Community/Junior College Quarterly of Research and Practice* 9 (1985): 27–36.

Brint, Steven, and Jerome Karabel. *The Transformation of the Two-Year College.* New York: Oxford University Press, forthcoming.

Clark, Burton R. "The Cooling Out Function Revisited." In *Questioning the Community College Role*, edited by G. Vaughan. New Directions for Community Colleges Series, no. 32. San Francisco: Jossey-Bass, 1980.

_____. *The Open Door College.* New York: McGraw-Hill, 1960.

Cohen, Arthur, and Florence B. Brawer. *The American Community College.* San Francisco: Jossey-Bass, 1982.

_____. *The Collegiate Function of Community Colleges.* San Francisco: Jossey-Bass, 1987. See especially Chapter 5: "The Transfer Function: Making the Connection to Four-Year Institutions."

_____. "Transfer and Attrition Points of View: The Persistent Issues." *Community and Junior College Journal* 52 (December-January 1981–82): 17–21.

Cohen, Arthur, et al. *Transfer Education in American Community Colleges.* Los Angeles: Center for the Study of Community Colleges, 1985.

Donovan, Richard A., Barbara Schaier-Peleg, and Bruce Forer. *Transfer—Making It Work: A Community College Report.* Washington, D.C.: American Association of Community and Junior Colleges, 1987.

Dougherty, Kevin J. "The Politics of Community College Expansion: Beyond the Functionalist and Class-Reproduction Explanations." *American Journal of Education* 96 (May 1988): 351–393.

Eaton, Judith S. "Community College Culture." *Community and Junior College Journal* 55 (August-September 1984): 52–55.

Fairweather, Malcolm, and Mary E. Smith. *Facilitating the Transfer Process: The Need for Better Articulation between Two- and Four-Year Colleges.* ERIC Document ED 263 934. Plattsburgh, N.Y.: Center for Earth and Environmental Science, State University of New York–Plattsburgh, 1985.

Friendlander, J. "An ERIC Review: Why is Transfer Education Declining?" *Community College Review* 8 (Fall 1980): 59–66.

Furniss, W. Todd, and Marie Martin. "Toward Solving Transfer Problems: Five Issues." *Community and Junior College Journal* 44 (February 1974): 10–15.

Gregg, William L., and Patricia M. Stroud. "Do Community Colleges Help Salvage Late Bloomers?" *Community College Review* 4 (Winter 1977): 37–41.

Harmon, John P. "The Value-Added Effects of Community College Transfer Programs." Ph.D. diss., University of North Carolina–Chapel Hill, 1976.

Kintzer, Frederick C., ed. *Improving Articulation and Transfer Relationships.* New Directions for Community Colleges Series, no. 29. San Francisco: Jossey-Bass, 1982.

Kintzer, Frederick C., and Richard C. Richardson, Jr. "The Articulation/Transfer Phenomenon." *Community, Technical and Junior College Journal* 56 (February-March 1986): 17–21.

Kintzer, Frederick C., and James L. Wattenberger. *The Articulation/Transfer Phenomenon.* Washington, D.C.: American Association of Community and Junior Colleges, 1985.

Knoell, Dorothy M., and Leland Medsker. *From Junior to Senior College: A National Study of the Transfer Student.* Washington, D.C.: American Council on Education, 1985.

London, Howard. *The Culture of a Community College.* New York: Praeger, 1978.

Menacker, Julius. *From School to College: Articulation and Transfer.* Washington, D.C.: American Council on Education, 1975.

Moore, Katherine M. "The Transfer Syndrome: A Pathology with Suggested Treatment." *NASPA Journal* 18 (September 1981): 22–28.

Networks. *New Initiatives for Transfer Students: Urban Community College Transfer Opportunities Program.* New York: Ford Foundation, 1984.

Orfield, Gary, et al. *The Chicago Study of Access and Choice in Higher Education.* Chicago: Committee on Public Policy Studies, University of Chicago, 1984.

Phlegar, Archie G., Lloyd Andrew, and Gerald McLaughlin. "Explaining the Academic Performance of Community College Students Who Transfer to a Four-Year Institution." *Research in Higher Education* 15 (1981): 99–108.

Richardson, Richard C., Jr., and Louis W. Bender. *Helping Minorities Achieve Degrees: The Urban Connection.* A Report to the Ford Foundation. Tempe, Ariz.: National Center for Postsecondary Governance and Finance, Research Center at Arizona State University, 1986.

_____. *Students in Urban Settings: Achieving the Baccalaureate Degree.* ASHE/ERIC Higher Education Reports 1985:6. Washington, D.C.: Association for the Study of Higher Education, 1985.

Richardson, Richard C., Jr., and Donald S. Douchette. "The Transfer Function: Alive and Well in Arizona." *Community, Technical and Junior College Journal* 52 (May 1982): 10–13.

Richardson, Richard C., Jr., Elizabeth C. Fisk, and Morris A. Okun. *Literacy in the Open-Access College.* San Francisco: Jossey-Bass, 1983.

Roueche, John E. "Transfer and Attrition Points of View: Don't Close the Door." *Community and Junior College Journal* 52 (December-January 1981–82): 17, 21–23.

Walton, Karen Doyle. "Articulation: Transfer Agreements, Minimum Grades Acceptable on Transfer Courses, and Transferability of Associate Degrees." *Community/Junior College Quarterly of Research and Practice* 8 (1984): 169–184.

_____. "Transfer of Undergraduate Credit: The Quality and Quantity of Credit Accepted for Transfer." *College and University* 59 (Spring 1984): 217–228.

Warren, Jonathan. "The Changing Characteristics of Community College Students." *Renewing the American Community College: Priorities and Strategies for Effective Leadership.* San Francisco: Jossey-Bass, 1985.

Wattenberger, James L. "Junior and Community College Education." *Encyclopedia of Educational Research.* New York: Macmillan, 1982. 982–989.

Weis, Lois. *Between Two Worlds: Black Students in an Urban Community College.* Boston: Routledge and Kegan Paul, 1985.

Willingham, Warren W. *Access Problems: Transfer to the Upper Division.* AAHE/ERIC Research Report Number 2. Washington, D.C.: American Association for Higher Education, 1972.

Zwerling, L. Stephen. *Second Best: The Crisis of the Community College.* New York: McGraw-Hill, 1976.